SPACE JAMMIN'

Michael and Bugs Hit the Big Screen

Foreword by
Danny DeVito

Written by
Charles Carney
and
Gina Misiroglu

Photographs by
Bruce W. Talamon

RUTLEDGE
HILL PRESS

WORLDWIDE PUBLISHING

*To my mom, who knows nothing about
movies, basketball, or animation, but almost
everything about me.*
—CPC

To Michael, my friend and mentor,
—GM

Published in Nashville, Tennessee, by Rutledge Hill Press, Inc., 211 Seventh Avenue North, Nashville, Tennessee 37219.

Distributed in Canada by H. B. Fenn & Company, Ltd., 34 Nixon Road, Bolton, Ontario L7E 1W2. Distributed in Australia by Millennium Books, 33 Maddox Street, Alexandria NSW 2015. Distributed in New Zealand by Tandem Press, 2 Rugby Road, Birkenhead, Auckland 10. Distributed in the United Kingdom by Verulam Publishing, Ltd., 152a Park Street Lane, Park Street, St. Albans, Hertfordshire AL2 2AU.

Book designed by **David Kaestle.**
Associate designer **Rick DeMonico.**
Packaged by **David Kaestle, Inc.**, New York, New York.
Film separations by Final Film, Inc., Los Angeles, California.

Library of Congress Cataloging-in-Publication Data

Carney, Charles.
Space Jammin': Michael and Bugs hit the big screen/written by Charles Carney & Gina Misiroglu; photographs by Bruce Talamon; foreword by Danny DeVito.
    p.   cm.
    ISBN 1-55853-426-1 (hardcover)
    1. Space jam.   I. Misiroglu, Gina Renée.   II. Talamon, Bruce.   III. Title.
PN1997.S642C37 1996
791.43'72—dc20   96-31111

Printed in the United States of America.

1 2 3 4 5 6 7 8 9—99 98 97 96

Acknowledgments

It takes a lot of people in a lot of places to pull together a book of this magnitude. We would like to acknowledge the following people, without whose dedication and support this book would not have been possible: Michael Harkavy, vice president, Warner Bros. Worldwide Publishing, for providing us with the opportunity to write this book and for his mentorship throughout the creative process; Larry Stone, publisher of Rutledge Hill Press, for his sharp eyes; photographer Bruce W. Talamon for his extraordinary sensibilities and perspective; Jim Britt and Mike Jones, for their invaluable photo assistance; the design firm of David Kaestle, Inc., for their synergistic and incredibly talented approach to design and layout; Max Howard, president of Warner Bros. Feature Animation, as well as Ron Tippe, Tony Cervone, Bruce Smith, and Kay Salz, for their inexhaustible efforts on our behalf; the ever-patient Mitchell Ferm of Warner Bros. Feature Animation, who spent countless hours locating art and coordinating the images so precious to the content of the book; Allen Helbig, art director, Warner Bros. Worldwide Publishing, for his amazing illustrations and boundless humor; Michael Szymanski, for his many hours of research and interview support; producer Joe Medjuck of Northern Lights Productions, for his professionalism and generous donation of his time; Ken Ross; all the helpful folks at Cinesite — especially Ed Jones, Scott Dougherty, and Gilbert Gonzales — for their hand-holding guidance through the technical forest; Kathleen Helppie and Lorri Bond from Warner Bros. Classic Animation; Bill McD. and Mark and Georgia and Todd and Darlene for an extra ten ears; Nate Bellamy Jr., and Tim Grover, who made the Dome come to life; the technicians at the Warner Bros. stills lab and Leor Levine's Lemax Photo Group; magician Gabe Lakatosh and his computer wizards at Final Film; and the scores of people who gave generously of their time to be interviewed and provide quotes. Finally, without Skye Van Raalte-Herzog, Priscilla's coffee in Toluca Lake, and our friend Lorem Ipsum holding everything together for us on an hourly basis, this book would have been just another bright idea.

Contents

① WARM-UPS

Icon meets icon on the road to feature films ⑭

②

SHOOT ME NOW! SHOOT ME NOW!

A look at the live-action shoot, from the other side of the camera ㊿⑥

③ DOME AWAY FROM HOME

Welcome to basketball Valhalla, Hollywood style ㊾④

4
MOVING PICTURES
Animation is more than pictures that move
110

5
WHEN WORLDS COLLIDE
The digital merger of live-action and computer graphics make Michael Jordan a multidimensional star
132

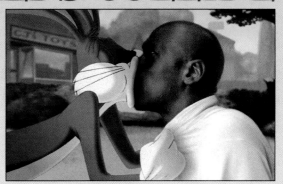

6
FINAL BUZZER
Sound effects, music, an NBA Championship — it all comes together
150

Outside Shot

by Ken Ross, *Space Jam* Executive Producer

"Hey Mike, we're going to try and put a movie deal together for you. Hope you won't mind sharing the star billing with Bugs Bunny and some other Looney Tunes characters. What do you think?"

"Sure, sure, go ahead, but I'm telling you guys, it feels like an outside shot," was Michael's brief retort. And so the game began.

David Falk and I really believed Michael Jordan could and should star in a full-length feature film. We had all worked together for many years on Michael's series of NBA videos and had seen him in countless commercials and interviews. He always seemed to be a natural in front of the camera. Moreover, Michael was a pop icon whose worldwide recognition extended far beyond the field of sports legends.

But Michael wasn't buying it. Not that he didn't want to make a movie, or that he lacked confidence in its success. It was his ultra-competitiveness. Michael hates to lose, and we'd all heard war stories about how hard getting a movie made in Hollywood is. Michael always carefully studies the odds and his ability to successfully influence the outcome. He doesn't like to commit his heart and mind to anything he doesn't think he can make happen.

Consider that Michael Jordan had never made a movie and Warner Bros. had never used their treasured Looney Tunes characters in a full-length feature film. Clearly we were talking about something pretty big and unusual.

As our negotiations with Warner Bros. progressed, we kept Michael informed and anxiously awaited the moment when he would let down his guard and celebrate — at least a little. But all we got was, "Sure, sure, when I'm on the set, then I'll believe it." Our biggest coup at one point was just getting Michael to say, "If you do pull off this deal, I'll show up."

David and I were extremely fortunate that Ivan Reitman and his Northern Lights Entertainment Company agreed to become our production partner. Then writers were sent to Birmingham to hang out with Michael and begin the script. Next, a director, Joe Pytka, was hired. He had previously worked with Michael on numerous commercials. The script was approved and finally the studio "green lit" the project.

As each of these major pieces fell into place, we'd call Michael to inform him and gloat a little. He was nonchalant about our progress and each time reminded us that when he was on the set with the cameras rolling, then it would be for real.

Along the way, we realized that Michael's intensive training for the 1995–96 season could not be compromised by the shooting of the film. So Warner Bros. built an incredible workout facility — a regulation basketball court, state-of-the-art weight room, and more. Two weeks before the start of principal photography, Michael was at the studio. I took him across the Warner lot to give him his first glimpse of what would be dubbed the "Jordan Dome."

He was very surprised. "Ken, this is really something else."

"They wouldn't have done this if it weren't for real, Mike," I answered. He quickly regained his game face and quipped, "Still an outside shot."

The day before the start of shooting, there was a complete script read-through for *Space Jam*. Everyone was there — Ivan Reitman, Joe Pytka, actors, cartoon voice talents, the writers, and the studio executives. I had to ask Michael, "Now, do you believe us?" He didn't miss a beat. "Not until I'm on the set."

Early the next day, we left the hotel, headed into makeup and wardrobe, and made our way to Stage 22 on the Warner lot. We stepped over cables, dodged technicians, met the crew, and joked with the people setting up the cameras and lighting for the cavernous "green screen" set. We were almost ready to roll when I couldn't resist jabbing my elbow in Michael's side. "Say, Mike, where are we?"

"Why are you asking? It's Burbank, isn't it?"

"No, that's not what I mean. Look around, where are we?"

He got it, smiled, and nodded. "I hear you," was all he said.

SPACE JAM™

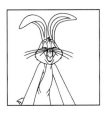

Foreword

by Danny DeVito

I can't believe somebody called me to write the foreword to a book. I worked *two whole days* on *Space Jam*. I read the script, yes. I thought it was cool, yes. Had a ball, okay. Ivan's crazy — it makes it easy.

Confession: My entire life, I've been a totally dedicated fan to the King of All Rascals. The vegetable muncher of all munchers. (Sing it: "Lut-dun-YUT-dun-YAH-da, lut-dun-YUT-dun-YAH-da! Oh, I'd rather have a carrot than a zebra or a parrot, 'cause a carrot is me very favorite lunch!") Ehhhh . . . What's up, Doc? What's cooking, King of the Underground, Skipper of the Light Fantastic? Ehhhh . . . To be, or not to be in a flick with the Fudd Fuddler? Hard to Pasadena, especially when there's another fly in the sky: Michael, how high (and ACCURATE) can you get? Every spin dunkin' doctor of roundballology wishes he could have a TENTH of the style and grace you wake up to. Ehhhh . . . *I'm in!* I have kids, you know. I like going to movies with my kids. I can't wait to see this movie.

There are great drawings (and photos) in this book of all the characters, living and animated. Of course, Swackhammer is my favorite — that's the guy whose voice I am. Did that make sense? I wonder how long forewords have to be? This is probably good though, right?

I'm proud to be a part of this.

Yours in celluloid,

Danny DeVito

Gamesmen

It's nearly impossible to think of Chicago without thinking of Michael Jordan, or to think of Warner Bros. without thinking of Bugs Bunny. No matter how intriguing the geography — from the city's stunning skyline to the studio's rows of soundstages where magic is created — it becomes a mere backdrop against which the stars themselves glow in bright relief.

It's hard to see a star directly. But if you move your eyes slightly to the left or right of it, it becomes more clear in the periphery. So it is with Michael and Bugs. Both are inexplicably famous, a fame that can be read more easily in the reactions they incite in others.

It's the stuff of entertainment and myth. Drama and delight. Man and rabbit. Peaceful by nature, unstoppable when pressed. Instinctive. Explosive. Cool. Elusive. Incandescent. Dazzling. Cutting through the yawning cynicism of an age to

suggest something sublimely human. Masters of their respective games.

As the movie *Space Jam* came to be, the brilliance of Michael and Bugs became even more clear through the actions and efforts of hundreds of creative people — directors, producers, writers, athletes, actors, animators, technical wizards, and craftsmen (all masters of *their* games) who pooled their skills. It's a funny, fantastic story about challenges and dreams, teamwork and heroes. Basketball players and animated characters. And all that's *behind* the camera.

This book is a pictorial essay on the hard-facts business of moviemaking. This complex universe, leavened with boisterous good humor, somehow manages to transcend the sum of its parts and to achieve the magical. *Space Jam* is the feature-film debut of both its stars, emissaries of two different but surprisingly parallel worlds.

Welcome to *Space Jam.*

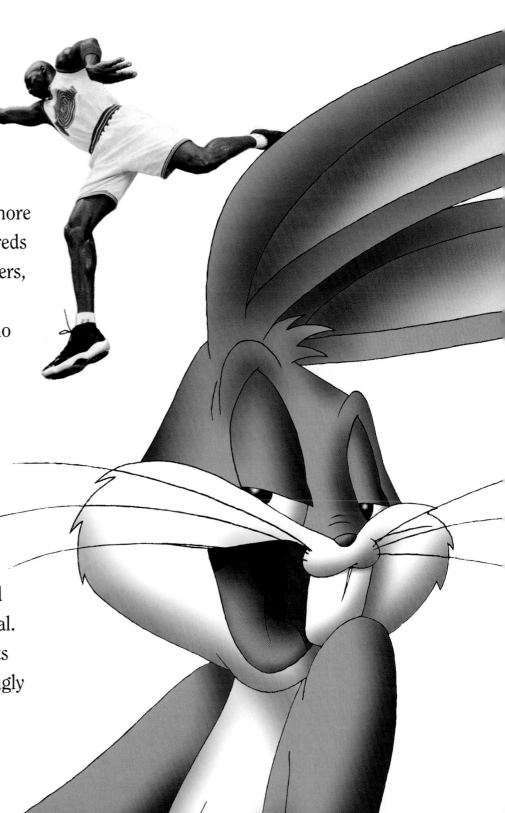

Interview

Q & A: Michael Jordan and Bugs Bunny

September 30, 1995. The Dugout, Blair Field, Long Beach, California. It's Michael Jordan's last day on the shoot at Long Beach's Blair Field, where the *Space Jam* crew is filming a baseball sequence. Michael, easily identifiable in his baseball uniform, watches as about four hundred people mill around in the stands, some holding up signs. Bugs Bunny is also lounging in the dugout, staying in the background as Jordan is interviewed, although Bugs never stays in the background for long.

Q: First, I want to ask you about one of your favorite Warner Bros. characters. . . . Who do you most identify with? Is it Bugs?

MJ: Probably Bugs. I've done a lot of work with him (laughs). He's very, ah, clever, smart.

Q: And he's cool.

MJ: He's perfectly cool . . .

BB: Poifectly.

Without a change of expression, Bugs rests his foot on Michael's shoulder. Michael tries to ignore him.

MJ: . . . has his own personality. He goes back and forth. He could be the good guy, he could be the bad guy. You know, I tease people quite a bit.

BB: Say not so.

MJ: He loves to joke and pick at people.

BB: Blame it on Brooklyn. I'm a product o' me environment.

MJ: I'm from Brooklyn. I was born in Brooklyn.

Q: Did you know that Bugs was from Brooklyn?

MJ: (genuinely surprised) Uh, no, I didn't know that. That's the first I . . .

BB: Eh, small world, ain't it? I guess when you're six-five, everything's a small world.

Bugs kisses Michael on the top of his head. Michael puts his baseball hat on.

MJ: I knew he was a working class guy.

BB: Salt-o'-the-oith.

Q: Say, um, Bugs . . .

BB: Um. Anything else?

Q: You're sort of out of your element here, on the basketball court and all. How would you explain the difference between movies and basketball?

BB: One's runnin', leapin', sweatin', shovin', and yellin', and gettin' overpaid for it. The other one's basketball. Right, Mikey?

MJ: Well, acting is a special talent . . .

BB: Careful, Stretch. "Special" means "50 percent off."

MJ: . . . you have to know yourself and you have to know your inner feelings quite a bit. Basketball? Physically, it's demanding. It's not as much emotion as it is talent.

BB: (mock indignant) So, eh, whattya tryin' to say?

MJ: It's a whole different understanding of yourself. You deal more with your feelings in acting and more with your talent in basketball.

BB: Nice catch, Mr. Berra.

Jordan laughs. Bugs hops down onto the bench next to him and is interested in the interview now. He leans his arm on Michael's

shoulder as he speaks and chews a carrot about two inches from his ear, which Michael clearly doesn't like, and he gently pulls away.

Q: Bugs, were you worried about the athletic demands of the role?

BB: Nah. I've played baseball, boxed, wrestled, raced a turtle (twice), been in the Foreign Legion, and had dinner at the American Legion. You've gotta be in good shape for that.

Q: What would you say to another animated character who thinks he's going to make the switch to professional basketball?

BB: Take up cribbage.

MJ: Bugs is a ham . . .

BB: You're thinkin' of Porky . . .

MJ: (clears his throat and looks at Bugs) . . . I think he's very relaxed in front of people and [he] knows how to entertain. We both enjoy our jobs. Only difference is, I don't like carrots.

BB: Glad to hear it. One food item I don't have to guard wit' my life around these guys.

Q: How do you compare playing professional basketball to playing with the Monstars?

MJ: It's different, you know, to be part of something new and risky . . . a lot of dangers, but I think the whole script, and the way [the Monstar players] are portrayed, is fun. I think you're going to hate them at first, but then you may like them at the end. I think that's something kids are going to find very appealing.

BB: Diplomatic corps for you, mister.

Q: Are you making a message movie here?

BB: Oh, yeah. It's the eternal struggle between good and evil, right and wrong, nature versus nurture, to-may-toe and to-maw-toe.

MJ: (laughs) You know, I think that there might be something to that, because kids will find something in it that's very appealing, a message of teamwork and overcoming the bad guys with it. We can learn a lot from the Monstars and their mistakes.

Q: What's most difficult is that people don't realize how hard it is to play Michael Jordan. You're actually playing yourself.

MJ: Well, I thought it would be easier.

BB: I thought it would be easier, too. Playin' Michael Jordan, that is. Michael does all his own stunts, y'know.

Q: The biggest rumor I've heard about you on this set is that Michael Jordan's height is six feet five and not six feet six.

MJ: You can quote six-five.

Q: Bugs, have you heard any rumors you'd like to clear up here?

BB: Nope. But if ya hear any good ones, I hope you'll pass 'em along. I'll pay ya if ya get 'em to the right people.

1

**It takes vision to make a great movie.
Vision and sweat. A pair of American legends doesn't hurt either.
Eat your carrots and keep your eye on the ball. This is
the story of the high-impact warm-ups it took to get into the
game of *Space Jam*.**

Sweat

Rumors had been circulating the halls of Warner Bros. Feature Animation for a long while that Michael Jordan was negotiating to costar in a movie with Bugs Bunny, but no one was taking them seriously. After all, Jordan was retired from basketball, playing only what could be kindly described as modest minor league baseball, which was taking some of the sheen off his myth.

The overall tenor of the comments was similar: The movie can't hurt *Jordan*, but what's it gonna do to *Bugs Bunny*?

After the enthusiastically received, Warner Bros.–assisted Nike commercial in 1991, there was no question that Jordan and Bugs were a good team. But that was a commercial. Sixty whole seconds. Even the worst marriages can sustain interest for a minute. But how was this going to hold up over an hour and a half? On a huge screen. With paying customers who will actually have to leave their living rooms to see it.

Besides — Looney Tunes in a feature-length film? Won't work. No way. Forget it. The Looney Tunes characters *made* the six-minute format. The compression of six minutes allowed the popular Warner Bros. "shorts" a tension and bounce that won't translate to a ninety-minute film. Decompress them and you'll kill them. That's their environment. That's where they work.

The Looney Tunes (and Merrie Melodies) had been at first nothing more than charming little confections built around a song, subcontracted by producer Leon Schlesinger to promote Jack and Harry Warner's sheet music publishing.

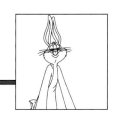

An Animated Cast of Characters

Starring:
Bugs Bunny

Also Starring:
Daffy Duck
•
Sylvester the Cat
•
The Tasmanian Devil
•
Porky Pig
•
Wile E. Coyote
•
Road Runner
•
Elmer Fudd
•
Yosemite Sam
•
Pepe Le Pew
•
Tweety
•
Foghorn Leghorn

And Introducing:
Lola Bunny

But in the summer of 1940, the tone of these confections took a bold hop forward in a routine Tex Avery short called "A Wild Hare," starring a smart-alecky rabbit named Bugs Bunny. This appearance of the rabbit (who had been used twice before to no great effect) galvanized his character with moviegoers. From the beginning, Bugs was no cartoon character. He was a star, a two-dimensional character with a four-dimensional personality.

Bugs was in good company with Daffy Duck and Porky Pig, and they were joined quickly by a veritable menagerie of memorable characters who reflected the personality traits — good and bad — of real human beings. Rather than play it safe, the creators of the Looney Tunes preferred their stars to be upstarts, rebellious and defiant. Anarchy made fun.

The Looney Tunes aren't so much "in your face" as conspiratorial. With a wisecrack, a simple arch of the eyebrow, or a kick in the pants, they invite the audience to the party. Conveniently and outrageously, they are flexible and instantly regenerative, at least in the anatomical sense. When the anvil tolls for Wile E. Coyote, he's back (in perfect shape) ten frames later. When Yosemite Sam's petard gives him hoist, he shakes it off in a second. The only thing that lingers is the humiliation, not the lesson. Their violence hurts them, certainly, but not in the same way ours hurts us, which keeps the comedy from being appalling. The Warner Bros. cartoon directors understood this. Children understand this.

Producer Ivan Reitman grew up on Warner Bros. cartoons, and the humor of his films is informed to a degree by the antics of Bugs Bunny and his animated cronies. Reitman, whose successes with *Animal House* and *Ghostbusters* (among many other films) have made him one of Hollywood's creative elite, was directing *Dave* at Warner Bros. in 1993. On a flight with a Warner Bros. executive, Reitman listened as the conversation casually moved to the topic of a Michael Jordan/Bugs Bunny movie. "[Warner Bros.] said that they were interested in expanding and creating a real movie for Jordan and the Looney Tunes," Reitman, who describes himself as a "huge basketball fan" and a longtime fan of the Looney Tunes, recalls.

"They were looking for something that could be created for a combination live-action and animated film that would capture the spirit of the Looney Tunes and still work as large-scale entertainment. I thought, *Why not?*" After his promotional commitments for *Dave* were satisfied, he began working on what was then labeled "the Michael/Bugs movie."

Dan Romanelli, who heads up the powerful Warner Bros. Consumer Products division, remembers that at first the studio liked the idea of *Space Jam* "but it wasn't something they could put their arms around." Romanelli expressed his support for the project at its inception, recognizing its enormous commercial possibilities. Still, with a nebulous story and no director or producer chosen, there was no way to get it moving until Reitman agreed to produce the film and bring in his creative group. "Ivan really made it happen — he got the top management excited about it and made the whole project go [forward]," Romanelli explains.

Reitman's commitment was the creative push that David Falk and Ken Ross had been waiting for. Falk and Ross also grew up in the generation for whom Saturday mornings meant Looney Tunes cartoons on television. Ross has been a close business associate of Falk and Michael Jordan since the late 1980s, making inroads on Jordan's behalf into the entertainment business. It started with a series of home videos based on

READY TO TAKE IT TO
THE RACK, JACK!

YOSEMITE WHIPS OUT GUNS
"I PITY THE FOOL THAT HAS
TO GUARD ME"

WE'RE GONNA TOAST EM...
BAKE EM

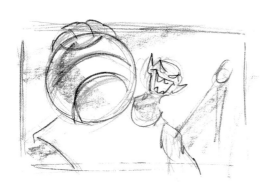

Michael's greatest on-court moments as well as glimpses into his off-court life. Falk has been Jordan's lawyer/agent since the then-underestimated athlete left North Carolina.

Ross and Falk always believed that Jordan could make another kind of leap — into a major film career — if the project and its timing were right. Each video was a step toward Falk's and Ross's vision of a much bigger plan, small parts of a dream. "One of the notions was always to do a fantasy-based project, but the idea was never fleshed out, and home video or television budgets were never adequate for what we wanted to do," Ross explains. "I wanted [Michael] to have an event. But we thought less about the high concept and more about the importance of a great story, and a great creative partner to help pull it off."

Jordan had been offered many cameo roles in other people's movies, usually as — surprise — a basketball player. But he was adamant that his film debut be *his* vehicle. "[He's] got a fantastic sense of comedy and a great wit," says Ross, "a great sense of humor, and it was very important that he do a comedy."

For the Michael Jordan film project, context was everything. Simply put, there is no character that could be created in fiction bigger or more appealing than Jordan is in real life. "We've always felt," Ross recalls, "that Michael should play himself in the picture. [He's] a pop icon, a superstar, and a character audiences are interested in seeing. So why create a new character for Michael Jordan to portray when audiences want to see more of Michael Jordan, just in a different medium?"

The other thing that got Ross's and Falk's wheels turning was the notion of a long-form Jordan/Bugs performance, a teaming that Warner Bros. had already given its blessing. "What better form of a 'buddy movie' could you have? If you look at the two of them, they have so much in common that it's a natural they [should] work together in the movies." Falk and Ross negotiated an open-ended deal for Jordan with Warner Bros. Reitman stepped in at this point and began assembling, piece by piece, the team that could fulfill his vision for the film. He and his longtime creative colleagues, Joe Medjuck and Dan Goldberg, met with a writing duo and started pulling together a story.

At the same time, some of the Looney Tunes' top animators were moved from the studio's Classic Animation department and temporarily installed in a stripped-down editor's room at Reitman's Northern Lights offices on the Universal Studios backlot, where they were to begin "boarding" the still nebulous story.

By chance, screenwriting partners Steve Rudnick and Leo Benvenuti, creators of *The Santa Clause*, were working — unhappily — on a television show being filmed at Universal. They heard about the Michael/Bugs movie through Goldberg. At their first meeting, Medjuck recalls, "They came up with the idea of Bugs pulling Michael through a hole while Michael was playing golf."

The whimsical outer space element threw the story into a new realm. "We came up with the notion, well, let's make him Michael Jordan," Benvenuti says, laughing, "captured by aliens." Rudnick, who seems to be able to complete and contradict his partner's thoughts at the same time (and vice versa), adds, "We came up with the idea of why he left [basketball] and what happened to him." No one had any inkling that Jordan would return to the game. "Leo and I just sat down and batted around a couple of ideas, and we came up with this little Alice in Wonderlandish kind of story."

Reitman had been concerned that Jordan's struggling baseball playing alone didn't make much of a script. Ross, however, thought that *was* the story, and invited the writers to Alabama to hang around with Jordan as he played for the Birmingham Barons, the farm team for the Chicago White Sox. They captured a sense not only of his personality and his speech patterns but the extraordinary fish-out-of-water story unfolding before them — the virtual messiah of professional basketball coming to minor league baseball and throwing the Barons and the community into an uproar, selling out tickets instantly, and filling the stadium with new fans who were there to see one thing — and it wasn't the Barons.

This became the alien abduction plot's seed: The fact that Michael wasn't playing basketball professionally made him immune to the aliens' attempts to steal his powers, as they did with other NBA players, to beat the Looney Tunes at a basketball challenge. Rudnick and Benvenuti wrote three drafts of a script, but then had to leave the project for other commitments. As it stood, the Looney Tunes were in a jam with some larcenous outer space creatures, and Michael was called on to get them out of it. The next pass at the script was handed over to Tim Harris and Herschel Weingrod, the writers of *Trading Places*, who had worked with Reitman on *Kindergarten Cop* and *Twins*. They took Rudnick and Benvenuti's draft and struggled with it for months. The movie's "hook" seemed to be missing — something to drive the script and give it a sense of urgency.

"The big question was 'Will people know who Michael Jordan is two years from this meeting?' because he could be playing two more years of nonstellar baseball," says Harris, the courtly, soft-spoken half of the duo.

"Will they actually care who Michael Jordan is?" adds Weingrod, an athletic-looking straight talker. Fortune seemed to provide an answer to the dilemma. While Harris and Weingrod labored over yet another draft of the script, Michael Jordan announced his return to basketball. People cared.

In the ensuing frenzy (stock values for five Jordan-advertised businesses rose over $2 billion within three days of the announcement), the Michael/Bugs movie was now a top priority, driving through the middle of the other pending Warner Bros. Feature Animation projects like one of Jordan's trademark offensive plays. Baseball suddenly became an "incidental part of the story" according to Harris. Basketball, and the fantastic reason for Michael's historic return to the game, became the missing hook.

The animators in the Northern Lights editing room had already begun boarding the script as other artists at Warner Bros. Feature Animation designed the characters of the Nerdlucks, the Monstars, Swackhammer, and Looney Tunes' newest character (and female lead), Lola Bunny. The artists could hardly imagine that, within a few months, their legion would swell to over six hundred, drawing at a feverish pace in animation studios from Los Angeles to Ohio to Canada to England in order to meet what seemed an impossible deadline.

OUR KIDS BELIEVE IN BUGS BUNNY LIKE THE EASTER BUNNY AND SANTA CLAUS.

— *Juanita Jordan*

With a completed script, artists planning the look and execution of the animated sequences, and the special effects house, Cinesite, brought aboard, *Space Jam* had swung into full production.

In a year's time, the unlikely little project that few people took seriously had expanded into one of the studio's most highly anticipated blockbusters. The hard work of getting the players in place was done. Soon, this would all seem like the easy part of the job. No one in the animation department was smirking about the Michael/Bugs movie anymore.

Developing characters

In his first cartoon, Sylvester's name was Thomas. Speedy Gonzales had a gold tooth in his debut. Daffy, before he became the declarative, self-centered duke of one-downsmanship, was an explosive, water-bouncing loonatic whose only outstanding trait was his inability to contain his own impulses. For his first appearance, Pepe Le Pew was a fake-French skunk named Henry with a wife and family. Elmer Fudd seemed to change appearance in each of his first few cartoons. So it is with the development of characters, a trial and error process that is as valuable in discovering what doesn't work as what does.

The character designs chosen for the Looney Tunes in *Space Jam* are a blend of the old with the new. This is the Bugs of the late 1940s, the energetic rabbit who is still not so self-possessed that he can't experience fear. Daffy looks more like a duck, with a definite duck-like body shape, a more exaggerated beak, and more top feathers on his head. Tweety's head, feet, and eyes are bigger, which heightens his wide-eyed innocent look. Foghorn is the hyperactive, speak-with-his-hands rooster from his earliest cartoons. The choices are deliberate, a calculated throwback to the characters' youth, mixed with the familiarity of the years spent before an audience. It's as if they've come back from retirement — rested, recharged, and ready for the future — like one of their human *Space Jam* costars.

Yosemite Sam is an outlaw, no matter how he's dressed. Tiny, loud, and irascible, he was rumored to be a reflection of Friz Freleng, who directed all the Yosemite Sam cartoons.

No matter how he looks, Elmer Fudd is a knucklehead. Like Bugs, Daffy, and Sam, Elmer has had a number of redesigns during a career in which everything evolved but his brain.

Bugs Bunny changed from a round-snouted wise guy in 1940 to a more slender and expressive wise guy in 1996.

Daffy began as a hyper-frenetic crazy but became more of a thinking-man's duck under Chuck Jones's direction, with his original low center of gravity stretching and shifting its shape (as does his bill) over the years. In *Space Jam*, he's back to being low in the bottom again.

Q & A: DAFFY DUCK

February 29, 1996. Priscilla's Coffee, Toluca Lake, California.
Although he turns sixty in 1997, Daffy looks twenty and acts eleven.

Q: How did you get involved with *Space Jam*?

A: Serendipity, my lad. Serendipity. I've known Ivan and Joe for years, so when they signed the Jordan kid for a picture, they needed somebody to spice up the box-office appeal, and I got the call.

Q: Really? That's not what Ivan told me.

Long pause. Daffy mumbles something into the air.

Q: I'm sorry?

A: (softly but deliberately) I, um, auditioned. Espresso? Loosens the beak. Woo-hoo!

Q: No, thanks. Did you say you *auditioned* for a part in a Looney Tunes movie?

A: Truth be known, yes.

Q: Wasn't that a little . . . embarrassing? I mean, who *else* could play you?

He slaps his hand on the table.

A: Precisely and exactly! The trade ad said: "Daffy Duck-type actor needed for major studio release." Of course, they thought, I should be *flattered* to be seen as a *type*, probably saw it as a means to draw me out of retirement.

Q: You're *retired*?

A: Spare me the pious disbelief for a second, Ruggles. Of *course* I'm not retired. It's a hook — a draw.

Q: Hmmm . . . and it worked?

A: Obviously. At the third callback, I had Reitman eatin' out of my hand.

Q: *Third* callback?

A: It was between me and a guy from the Groundlings. I read from the Song of Solomon and there wasn't a dry eye in the house. Sorry — napkin?

Q: Yes, thank you. Would you mind turning your beak away ever so slightly when you use S-words?

A: Certainly! Whoops! C-word! Woo-hoo! Here, use mine.

Q: Thank you.

A: Espresso? What? What? *Another* napkin?

Q: Never mind.

25

SWACK. ATTITUDE SUGGESTIONS

Swackhammer emerges from concept to form

Concept sketches create a starting point for evaluating how a character's look best suits his or her personality as it is written in the script. In a sense, it is the visual casting process for all animated characters. Swackhammer, villainous CEO of Moron Mountain, has undergone several permutations — from a narrow, caped, Basil Rathbone-ish scoundrel of early sketches to music hall manager, to becrowned rajah, to sandal-clad, bloated thug. It was necessary for his character, while remaining comical, to pose a true threat to Michael Jordan and the Looney Tunes. This was pulled off partly through a bursting-capacity suit and Swackhammer's huge, menacing hands.

Swackhammer Speaks!

On Freedom of Speech:
"Shut up!"

On Closing a Sale:
"You'll be our star attraction. You'll sign autographs all day long and play one-on-one with the paying customers. And you'll always LOSE! Do we have a deal?"

On Good Sportsmanship:
"Choke artists!"

On Hospitality:
"What'd you say? What if they can't come? Make 'em!"

On His Word:
"I lied."

The birth of a new comic species

Part of the difficulty in developing the tiny alien creatures known as Nerdlucks (Ivan Reitman's made-up nickname for them that stuck) was that they had to look like Looney Tunes characters and believably transform into the formidable Monstars. The initial sketches depict them as tiny spacemen, who then evolve into a band of dinosaur-like beings. Gradually they become variations of one species, unified by the similarity of their eyes, their sprung antennae, and their bow ties. The huge eyes, which contrast with insect-inspired bodies, make them appear desperate and vulnerable. When they threaten to abduct the Looney Tunes, the glee they express as captors plays off of their comically diminutive, bullied stature.

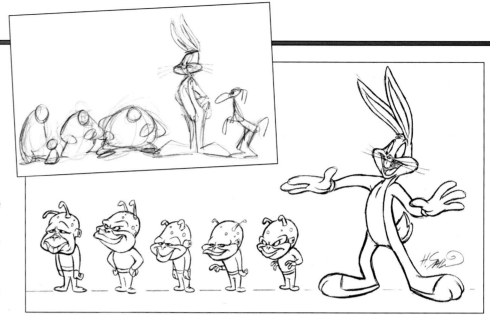

Colors, size relationships, and attitudes are the key links between the Nerdlucks — Bang, Bupkus, Blanko, Pound, and Nawt — and their alter-egos, the Monstars.

The image of the pint-sized Nerdlucks throwing their weight around is one of the comic highlights of *Space Jam*.

Away from the bullying Swackhammer, the normally timid Nerdlucks get a taste of power and run with it.

When Nerdlucks go bad

The transformation of the comical Nerdlucks to evil Monstars took months of design work. The first sketches show gooney adaptations of the hayseed foils of the 1940s Warner Bros. cartoons: one pigeon-toed, one buck-toothed, one sporting a lightbulb growing out of his head, another with a long, E.T.-style neck. The drawings prompted plenty of giggles, but there was something about them that wasn't exactly right. Just making them bigger wasn't enough — the Monstars lacked menace. In subsequent sketches, the villains began to take on more bulk and muscle, and their faces grew nastier-looking. They ultimately became a formidable challenge to Michael Jordan. They can practically fly and are able to shred a basket with a slam dunk. Their expressions — empty-eyed and savage — let the audience know that the Looney Tunes are in serious trouble.

Nawt is lean and fast, much smaller than his teammates, but with a streamlined, reptilian flexibility.

Early concept drawings of Blanko emphasize his heavy brow and pointed, largely vacant head; another incarnation plays up his long upper lip, emphasizing a loose and inarticulate mouth. While the brow on the final design is still thick and low, Blanko's forehead has been lengthened and widened and his hair shortened. He now looks capable of just enough thought to be a real menace.

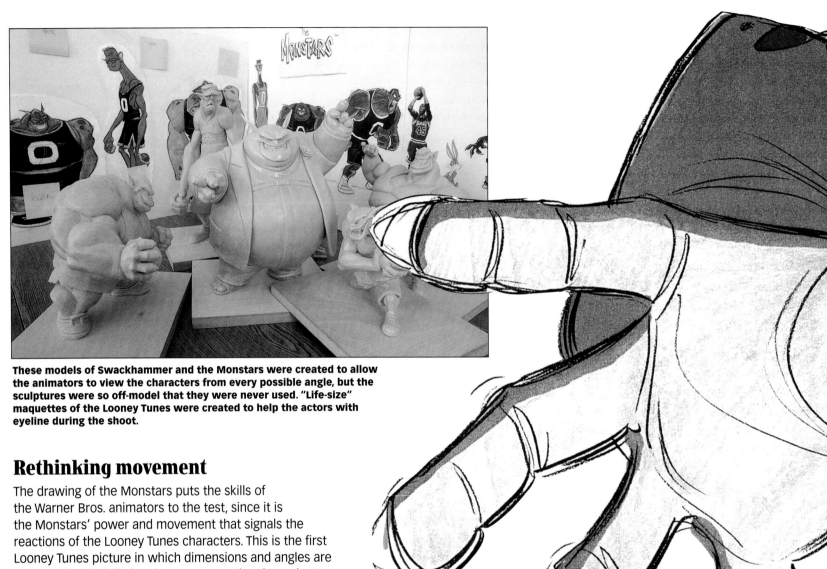

These models of Swackhammer and the Monstars were created to allow the animators to view the characters from every possible angle, but the sculptures were so off-model that they were never used. "Life-size" maquettes of the Looney Tunes were created to help the actors with eyeline during the shoot.

Rethinking movement

The drawing of the Monstars puts the skills of the Warner Bros. animators to the test, since it is the Monstars' power and movement that signals the reactions of the Looney Tunes characters. This is the first Looney Tunes picture in which dimensions and angles are stretched to their limits. These concept sketches adopt the kinds of angles that best show off the power of the Monstars. When they are pitted against the movements of Michael Jordan and Wayne Knight (through the moving-camera technique of director Joe Pytka), a whole new style of Looney Tunes animation is created. Characters move not only left to right but toward and away from the camera, with the camera itself moving around, above, and below them. It has forced a whole rethinking of the way the Looney Tunes are drawn.

Bullied no more!

Each of the Monstars bears the stamp of his Nerdluck incarnation, with the attitude of one who isn't about to be pushed around again. Ever. The Monstars behave like beasts yet move with the grace and skill of their NBA victims. There is nothing in their being to suggest the timidity of the Nerdlucks, only the savage joy of dominating and destroying. Animation producer Jerry Rees and director of animation Bruce Smith created the final models of the Monstars and Nerdlucks.

Timid as he looks, the Nerdluck lieutenant Bang is mean and nasty to a fault, and proud of it. He would love to be the head Nerdluck, and practices toward that goal. To call him a "big bully" as a Monstar would be an understatement of epic proportions, like the dimensions of his body.

Bupkus, as a Nerdluck, enthusiastically echoes and endorses every idea and thought that he hears. He has to. He has none of his own. As a Monstar, he loves his work, executing it — and his victims — with the same enthusiasm.

Nawt is the tiniest of the Nerdlucks, but his intelligence more than makes up for his size. Nawt is cute and wide-eyed on the outside, but he is still scheming at the core. And though he's small for a Monstar, he's slim and swift and all over the place — and definitely in your face.

Pound is the leader of the Nerdlucks. Either side of his bed is the wrong side. A wide-bodied, tiny tyrant-in-training, Pound is determined to throw his weight around — what there is of it. As a Monstar, he's still the leader, but now he's got the weight to throw around.

Blanko is just along for the trip, but he forgot to pack his brain. The tallest of the tiny, he's a surfer dude looking for the perfect wave — in the middle of the desert. As a Monstar, he's dumb taken to new heights. For one so tall, a lot goes over his head.

"Don't ever call me doll!"

The Looney Tunes characters, with a few exceptions, have been pretty much of a boy's club since 1930. Reitman and company were determined to come up with a love interest for Bugs, which arrived in the character of Lola Bunny. Tony Cervone, co-director of animation, remembers that she was "a lot more tomboyish at first, but it didn't take us long to figure out, 'Well, what do you do with *that*?' They always wanted Bugs to be totally gaga over her, so we kind of pumped her up more in the feminine attributes department." In between her initial look and the final model in the film, it's clear that she ended up, wisely, somewhere in the pendulum arc between tomboy and vixen.

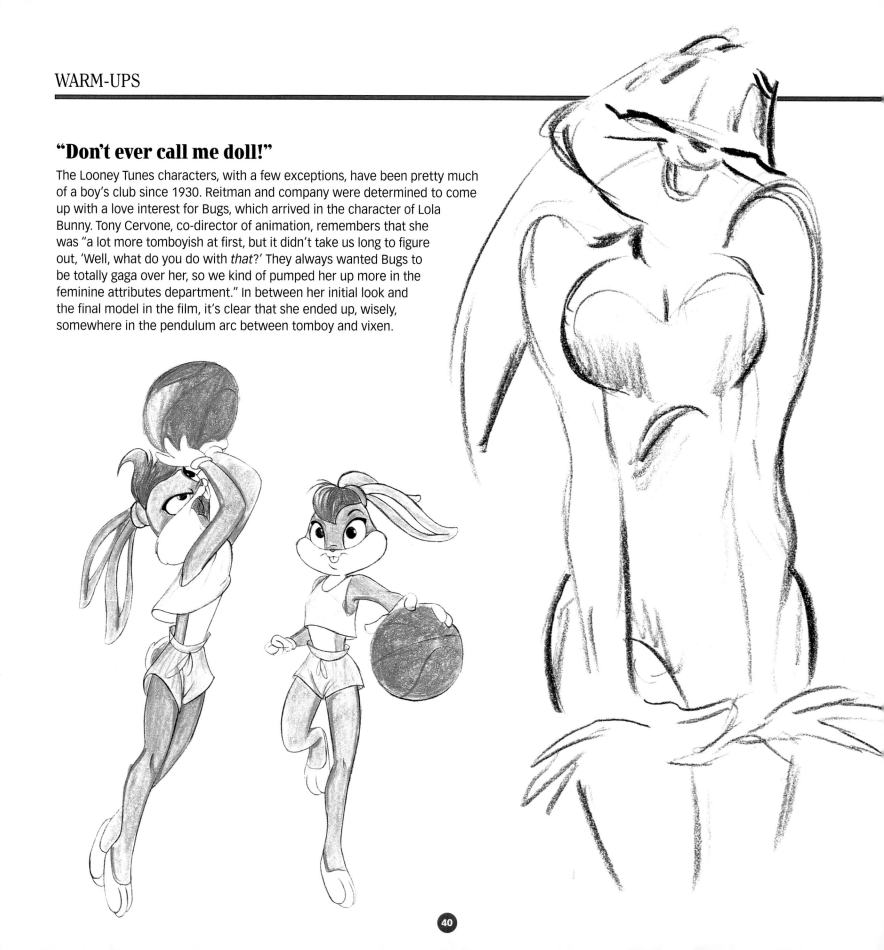

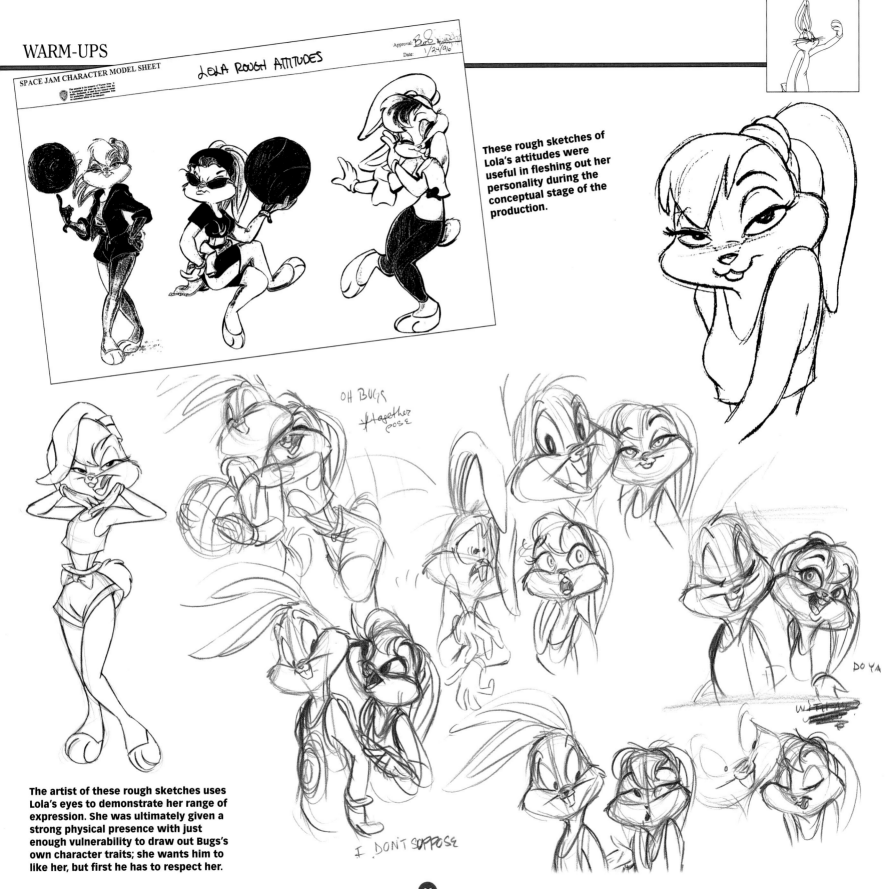

Approval: Bob [signature]
Date: 1/24/96

SPACE JAM CHARACTER MODEL SHEET

LOLA ROUGH ATTITUDES

These rough sketches of Lola's attitudes were useful in fleshing out her personality during the conceptual stage of the production.

OH BUGS
#Together pose

I DON'T SUPPOSE

DO YA

The artist of these rough sketches uses Lola's eyes to demonstrate her range of expression. She was ultimately given a strong physical presence with just enough vulnerability to draw out Bugs's own character traits; she wants him to like her, but first he has to respect her.

Words are worth a thousand pictures

A script is something of a roadmap to the final vision of the movie, although along the way many changes can be made by the writers, the producer, or the director. The script for *Space Jam* was originally written by Steve Rudnick and Leo Benvenuti, then revised and expanded by Tim Harris and Herschel Weingrod. Encouraged by Ivan Reitman, the animators were given free rein in creating gags for the animated characters. Often, under Reitman's guidance, voice actors performed ad lib lines that stayed in the film.

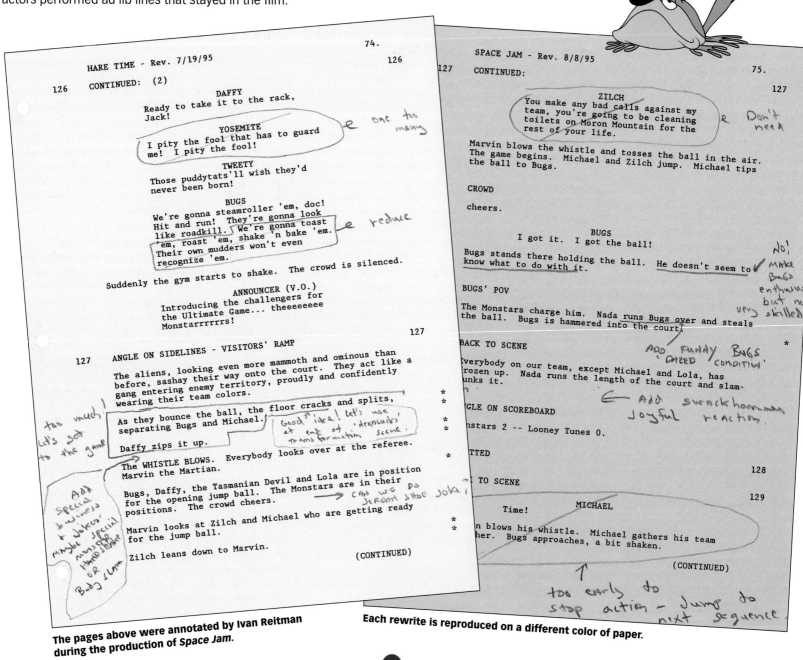

The pages above were annotated by Ivan Reitman during the production of *Space Jam.*

Each rewrite is reproduced on a different color of paper.

Interview

Q & A: Steve Rudnick and Leo Benvenuti

March 28, 1996. Los Angeles. Rudnick and Benvenuti were a stand-up comedy team in Chicago for fifteen years. Their latest screen credit is *The Santa Clause.*

Q: Did you use any specific [Looney Tunes] director as a touchstone for the way you were going to write this?

SR: Not really. As you write, you get a feel for the different Warner Bros. directors, and you can actually start picking up on [their style]. These guys really revolutionized the whole animated world. It's because of Warner Bros. that you have stuff like *Ren and Stimpy* these days — the eyes popping out of the head, breaking all the rules.

Q: Do you have a Looney Tunes character that you identify with?

SR: I was always kind of a [smart-alecky] kid, so of course I liked Bugs and his whole attitude.

LB: I like Bugs, but I think Daffy's a lot funnier. He's definitely underrated, suffering from the "second banana syndrome."

Q: Who has been the inspiration for you in your work?

SR: It's hard to say. I've always admired Albert Brooks and Woody Allen as writers. As a team we always admired Bob and Ray and were very much influenced by Monty Python, Peter Cook, and Dudley Moore, and the works of . . .

LB: . . . the works of Ivan Reitman (laughs).

SR: . . . uh, Peter Sellers, the whole *Goon Show* stuff.

LB: And mix in a little Italian absurdist theater and movies, De Sica, Fellini — they've always cracked me up.

SR: For me, it was the Yiddish theater (laughs).

Q: When you want to laugh, what do you turn to?

SR: I don't know — I like everybody. I like Albert Brooks a lot. You know what I'm watching recently are the Sgt. Bilkos *[Phil Silvers Show]*, and I'm on the floor, they were the funniest things. *The Honeymooners* . . . I grew up with a lot of these. I'm a lot older than Leo. I'm forty-four and Leo is thirty-five.

LB: I am?

SR: Write that down: "Steve was absolutely certain how old he was and Leo had no idea."

LB: I thought I was thirty-six.

SR: I want that in the book! On the record!

Storyboards: The script gets visual

Storyboards are an integral component of any action film and are absolutely necessary
in animation, where they originated. Here, the writer's dialogue and descriptive
passages are sketched as the camera might see them. It is from storyboards that an
animation director can follow the pacing of a script and make adjustments to the timing
of scenes before the very expensive and time-consuming process of animation
begins. Initially, the storyboard itself is shot on film, approximating the length
of each scene, with a dialogue track. This is called the "story reel."

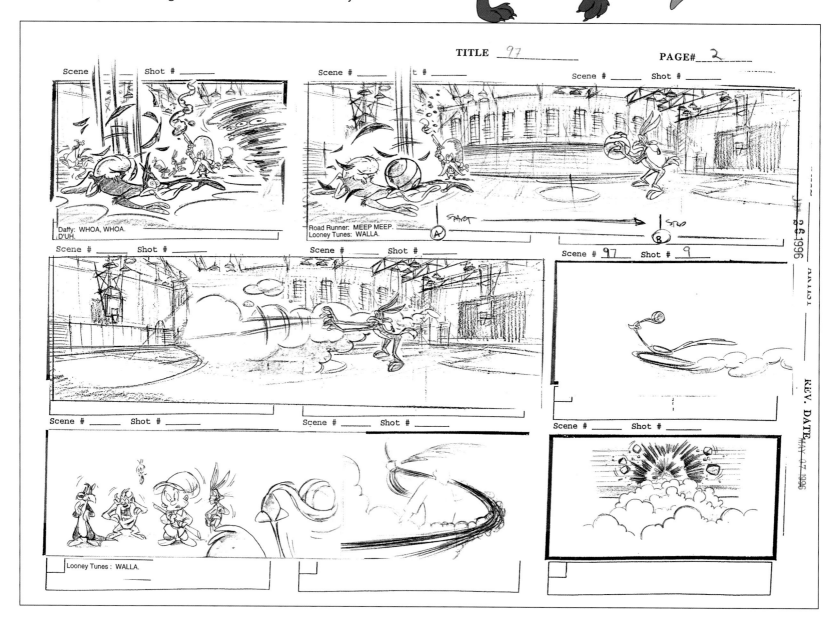

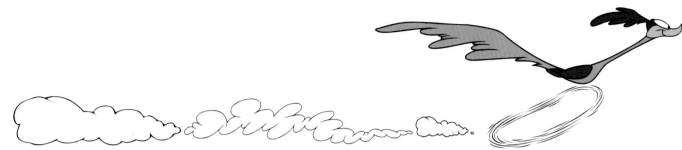

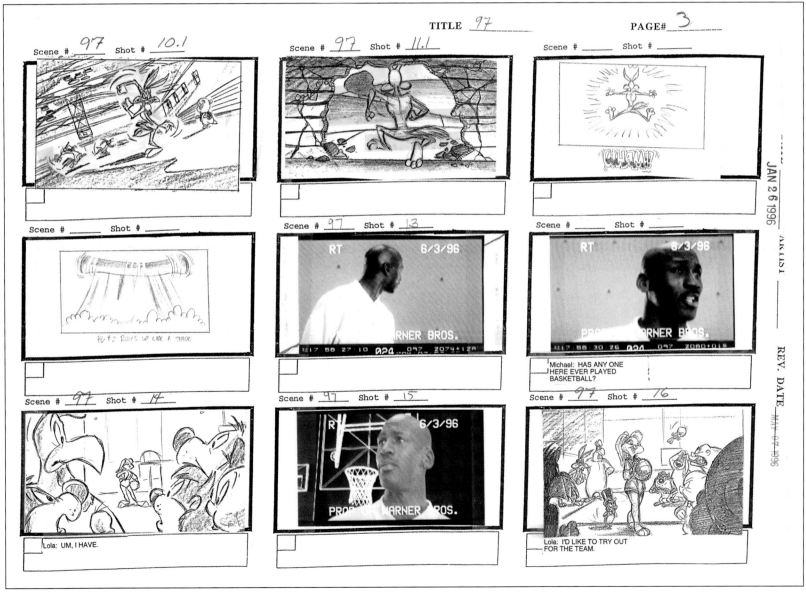

TITLE _97_   PAGE# _3_

Scene # _97_ Shot # _10.1_

Scene # _97_ Shot # _11.1_

Scene # _____ Shot # _____

JAN 2 6 1996

Scene # _____ Shot # _____

Scene # _97_ Shot # _13_

Scene # _____ Shot # _____

Michael: HAS ANY ONE HERE EVER PLAYED BASKETBALL?

Scene # _97_ Shot # _14_

Scene # _97_ Shot # _15_

Scene # _97_ Shot # _16_

REV. DATE MAY 07 1996

Lola: UM, I HAVE.

Lola: I'D LIKE TO TRY OUT FOR THE TEAM.

The reel story

Soundstage 22: During principal live-action photography, a team of animators on the set prints "thermal" images directly from the camera monitor and sketches in the position of the animated characters. This image is then inserted into the storyboards to give the director a focal point for directing the live-action actor, in this case Michael Jordan. As the animation is completed and "cleaned up" by an assistant animator, it is inserted scene-by-scene in the story reel, replacing the storyboard material.

The contrast between the storyboard sketches and the final film images is startling; what remains, ideally, is the rough energy and wit of the initial drawings.

M.J. "WE'VE GOT TO GET IT BUGS HOLD UP BOTTLE NOW FULL OF WATER.

M.J. "ARE YOU WITH ME OR NOT."

WIDE SHOT TOONS SLEEPING

BUGS: "LISTEN DOC THAT WAS A GREAT SPEECH...

...REAL INSPIRATIONAL — GO GET 'EM AND EVERYTHING — BUT DIDN'T YOU FORGET SOMETHING?" — M.J. "WHAT?"

BUGS: "YOUR SECRET STUFF DOC!" CAM. TRUCK

BUGS GULPS DOWN A SHOT OF THE "SECRET STUFF"

Scene # 141   Shot # 23

Clip # _____   Nerdlucks: WALLA.   Tnk # _____

Scene # 141   Shot # 24

142   1M

Scene # _____   Shot # _____

142   1N

Scene # _____   Shot # _____

141   13A

SCOOTER SKIDS TO STOP.

Scene # _____   Shot # _____

141   14

Bugs: SPECIAL DELIVERY.

TITLE SC 141 U.2/22

Scene # 141   Shot # 21

PAGE# 4

Scene # _____   Shot # _____

141   14A

2   BUGS TOSSES BALL

Scene # 141   Shot # 19

Scene # 141   Shot # 20

Shot # _____

A063

Clip # _____   Minions: BOO! WALLA
Swack: BOO!

Clip # _____

20   64

A063

PAN TO

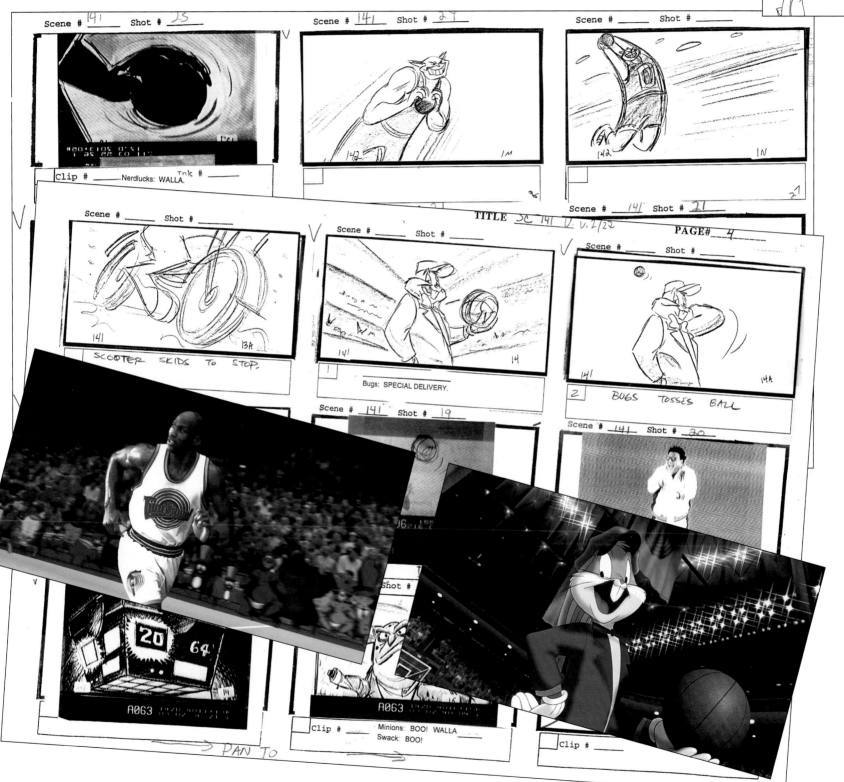

Designer dilemma

Moron Mountain is a key element in the film, and since it is the first animation on the screen, its design must establish the tone for the rest of the movie. The design choice is a challenge. In just forty-five seconds of film, Moron Mountain must be captivating and funny, but it can't look like so much fun that anyone would ever want to go there. Art director Bill Perkins and layout supervisor Gary Mouri considered several different approaches before selecting one that projects Moron Mountain's loopy but irritating atmosphere.

Art director Bill Perkins must select design elements, such as color and light sources, that will subliminally drive the movement and dialogue of the film without getting in the way of storytelling. It's a delicate balance.

Q & A: Bill Perkins

March 7, 1996. Sherman Oaks, California. The tall and lanky Perkins is a painter at heart, and he speaks with a painter's visual vocabulary.

Q: What drew you into animation?

A: I got involved with some other painters to try to do something bigger than just the edges of our canvases, a collaborative art form. The second film I worked on was *The Little Mermaid,* and that one made animation seem like something worth sticking around for.

Q: What's the responsibility of the designer?

A: You have to look at everything between the components [of the film's story]. You have to look at the logic between these components, and when you look at that, you can get your meaning across at a gut level.

Q: Example?

A: You can't look at all the leaves on the tree, you have to look at the whole tree and where it is. How does the light hit it, and how do the tree and the light relate to the other components? It's looking at the impression of the day rather than the elements alone.

Dumb fun

Moron Mountain is the initial introduction to the animated world of *Space Jam*, setting the stage for the film's key conflict. Because of this, a later rendition (right) is decidedly less whimsical than these early concept sketches. While blending stylings from the 1950s with a 1990s wryness, these drawings suggest more a

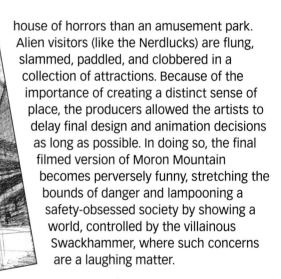

house of horrors than an amusement park. Alien visitors (like the Nerdlucks) are flung, slammed, paddled, and clobbered in a collection of attractions. Because of the importance of creating a distinct sense of place, the producers allowed the artists to delay final design and animation decisions as long as possible. In doing so, the final filmed version of Moron Mountain becomes perversely funny, stretching the bounds of danger and lampooning a safety-obsessed society by showing a world, controlled by the villainous Swackhammer, where such concerns are a laughing matter.

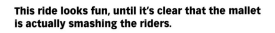

This ride looks fun, until it's clear that the mallet is actually smashing the riders.

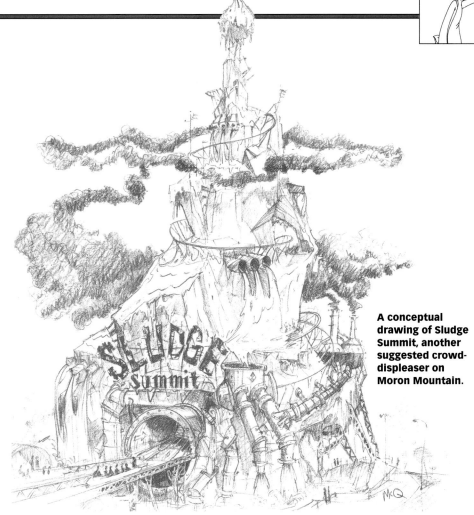

A conceptual drawing of Sludge Summit, another suggested crowd-displeaser on Moron Mountain.

PREMIERE

Background information

The only place where cheating is not only acceptable but *demanded* is in animation backgrounds. Here, the layout artist has designed some apparently sedate backgrounds for the action in Looney Tune Land. However, in the course of the action, ceilings rise, doorways move, and floor planes are skewed to create a more dramatic effect, all without the audience noticing. Layout artist Gary Mouri admits, "We go a long way, do a lot of cheating, but it works."

At the top is the layout artist's "tight pencil" drawing of the Looney Tunes' town hall. Above is the background artist's final color "key" for this same background.

Spit-shined

This is the practice gym where Bugs meets Lola — and the Monstars. The layout artist, using the storyboards as guides, sets the stage and style for an animated film's backgrounds. The background artist then takes the layout sketch and "color keys" it. The above image, rendered by computer, originated in the layout sketch.

2

SHOOT ME NOW! SHOOT ME NOW!

Dailies are the raw footage of filmmaking,
viewed at the end of a day's shoot. But what happens
on the other side of the camera?

Dailies

In any other basketball setting, this would be a disaster. Shawn Bradley is nursing a knee injury. Larry Johnson is careful not to aggravate his back, which stiffens so much his trainer swears that Johnson "can tell when it's going to rain." Patrick Ewing, cautious after two herniated disks, stretches for twenty minutes before practicing. Muggsy Bogues, on crutches, is recovering from recent knee surgery. In moviemaking, these are simply adjustments. "I saw the dailies and I looked fine," Bogues said, flashing his brilliant trademark smile. "They had me dribbling and the camera moved around and there was no problem. That's Hollywood, I guess."

Dailies are raw footage, reviewed at the end of the day's action. In the movie business, a project's "buzz" — the unofficial yea or nay on a film before it is finished — is often drawn from reactions to the dailies.

NBA players are camera-savvy young men. But what goes on outside the view of the camera reveals the players as people, unguarded, before the director yells "Action!"

September 19, 1995. CIGNA Hospital, Los Angeles.
Entering Shawn Bradley's trailer, a visitor first spots his size 16 ½ shoes. In order to see Bradley himself, the visitor must follow the legs back to the farthest part of the trailer's interior, where Bradley, seven-feet-six inches tall, relaxes between takes. "I can't stand up in here," Bradley says apologetically. "I just come in to sit down."

Today's scenes are shot on the hospital's fourth floor. A woman arrives in the admissions lobby with her six-year-old. "My son isn't feeling well," she tells a guard. "Is Michael Jordan here today?" she asks in the same breath.

"Not today," the guard answers politely. She sighs.

"He's not here today, baby," she tells the little boy, towing him out the door as the child — who has evidently recovered from his illness — peers over his shoulder. This is her second day here. The admissions staff has rebuffed at least a dozen people with "minor emergencies" who had hoped to catch a glimpse of the star. Jordan is in New York.

The players are incorrigible teasers. In the makeup room, Bogues turns his smile on the fearsome Ewing. "When I grow up, I want to be just like Patrick. He's so moral and grown-up. He's knocked his head so many times against the backboard he doesn't even get his own jokes!"

"Leave me alone!" Ewing shoots back in mock irritation.

"No stress, no press," smiles Bogues.

Larry Johnson has a trademark scowl that flashes a gold tooth — his game face — but he's not wearing it on the *Space Jam* set.

"You're going to powder me to death," he good-naturedly warns makeup artist Cyndi Reece-Thorne. "Athletes are supposed to sweat, and besides you don't want me sneezing all over the place. Then the director is going to blame you."

September 20, 1995. The Los Angeles Sports Arena.
The Sports Arena will become Madison Square Garden, then the Great Western Forum, then Madison Square Garden again. Some of the thirty-six or more players in these mock games are household names among basketball fans, players whose careers have inspired millions of

teenagers: A. C. Green, Marques Johnson, Jeff Malone, Alonzo Mourning, Tracey Murray, Sharone Wright, Pooh Richardson, and up-and-comers like Grant Hill, Reggie Wallace, Anthony Miller, Derek Strong, and Derek Martin.

"You have a lot of people from different generations of basketball, with legends like Marques Johnson," says NBA player Brad Wright. "My heroes growing up are here. Four or five years makes a difference in the basketball world, and you're in a different generation. So, in a lot of ways, this feels like a family reunion."

As Charles Barkley cuts up with Ewing and Danny Ainge on the court, Reitman plays headmaster to get their attention. The players shut up as if they were caught talking in class. Barkley's suddenly innocent expression makes the others break out in laughter.

Barkley, who has retreated to the stands to watch the action, sits among the extras. At first, he is not interested in talking to anyone. Then he chats amiably with a couple next to him but turns down their request for an autograph.

Some of the Los Angeles Lakers have speaking parts in a scene outside the locker room, but a minor crisis occurs when Nick Van Exel doesn't show (he had become ill). After three hours and several frantic phone calls, Ken Ross reaches Cedric Ceballos, who had played at the Jordan Dome the night before. As the contract is being drawn up with his agent, Ceballos is en route to the Sports Arena, arriving, according to Ross, "like the cavalry."

Vlade Divac and coach Del Harris are ebullient about being on the set. Three and a half hours and eight takes later, they're numb.

In the locker room, Marques Johnson ignites a debate by declaring Speedy Gonzales faster than the Road Runner. The room erupts with sides quickly drawn.

On the gym floor, Charles Barkley is supposed to make a lay-up, and after many successful rehearsals, the cameras start rolling. Danny Ainge passes the ball to him, and Barkley misses. "Them aliens got to me early!" he says loudly, hanging his head in mock shame.

September 22, 1995. Downtown Los Angeles.

Downtown Los Angeles doubles as Detroit: an exterior scene on a specially constructed basketball court. A couple of hundred curious passersby are here to watch Barkley play in a pick-up game with some young girls who beat him because he's lost his powers.

In the background, two tough-looking locals are sitting in a disgorged car seat watching the action and listening to a loud boom box. When Barkley has trouble hearing Pytka's direction, he hollers, "Turn that thing down — we're making a movie over here!" The two guys scramble for the off-button.

Action. Barkley dribbles the ball, but it hits his foot and rolls off. Pytka looks at the cameraman. Barkley reads the look. "Of COURSE I did that on purpose!"

The filming finally ends for the day. Pytka tells Barkley, who has been anxious to leave, "You can go home now. Don't cry, big guy."

"I don't cry," Barkley snaps.
Then he fakes as if he is crying.

September 25, 1995. The John Marshall High School gymnasium.

Some kids are ditching classes and others are hanging out windows to get a glimpse of the players, especially Michael Jordan. One kid hands Shawn Bradley a page from his homework to sign. "Well, all right, but don't think that's going to get you a better grade," Bradley admonishes him. Some kids offer their shirts to be autographed. Muggsy Bogues signs a girl's hand. Larry Johnson flashes his gold-toothed smile and the kids scream with excitement.

The versatile character actor Wayne Knight, who plays Michael's annoying but lovable sidekick, Stan Podolak,

wears his portable radio headset between takes. "Mandarin Chinese lessons for my next film," he tells someone, but it's actually the closing arguments of the O. J. Simpson trial. Knight listens constantly, keeping the crew updated.

At noon, there's a visit from Hideo Nomo, the then-rookie Dodger pitcher, who receives a riotous reception from the students. He is smiling, quiet, and polite. Nomo, a tall and dignified figure in suit and tie, looks Michael Jordan squarely in the eye, then bows his head slightly. "It's a real pleasure," Jordan says. Everyone is standing around not knowing what to say. After a brief conversation, the meeting is over.

Jordan and Larry Johnson compare hair lengths. Jordan rubs L. J.'s close-cropped scalp and his own bald

head at the same time. Later, Michael hugs Barkley, then licks his fingers and playfully begins to rub Barkley's scalp as if he's trying to clean it off.

Off-camera, the players practice shooting hoops. Once the cameras roll, though, nobody can hit a basket.

"Oh, we lost our powers again," Muggsy quips.

"Please let me get this," Larry Johnson prays as he aims his shot. He misses. "Cut!" yells the director.

They're ready to roll again, with Michael on camera.

"You got your lines, black Superman?" chides Charles Barkley.

"You got yours?" Jordan shoots back.

"You don't have to worry about me. I'm a professional," Barkley smiles.

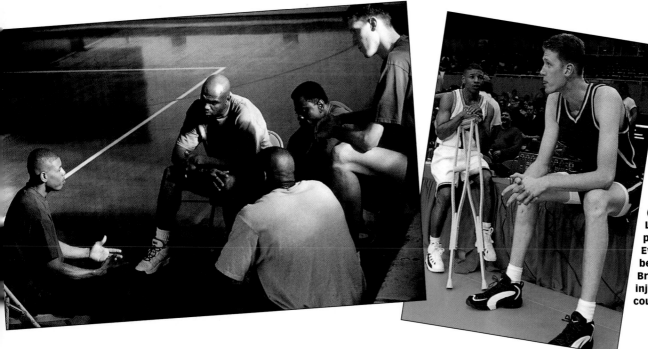

(far left) Ivan Reitman coaches Larry Johnson on how to play poorly; (middle) Bogues, Barkley, Ewing, Bradley, and Johnson chat between scenes; (left) Bogues and Bradley, both recovering from injuries, watch the Sports Arena court action from the sidelines.

Pytka has ordered a special set assembled off to the side of the Marshall gym to shoot Barkley's hospital scene, for which the star was absent at CIGNA Hospital. Barkley lies on the doctor's table, attached to tubes and machinery. Ewing can't pass up the chance for a dig.

"The line on this machine is just going to go straight," he laughs. "This man doesn't have a heart."

"You're done here today," Pytka tells Ewing.

Then Ewing throws a pillow at the crotch of the immobilized Barkley.

September 27, 1995. Soundstage 22, Warner Bros. Studios, Burbank.

Jordan is in position. Pytka yells, "Okay, roll 'em."

Three seconds into action. "Cut! Put your hands on your hips," Pytka orders Jordan.

"Did I have it that way before?" Jordan asks.

"Yes, you did."

"Are you sure?"

"Yes, I am," Pytka says.

"Go back and look at it. Are you sure, Morgan?" Morgan is the script supervisor who sits on a high stool next to Pytka at all times and keeps an eye on continuity throughout the movie. She nods.

"Rolling. Wait, wait, cut!" the director says. "Remember your hands, we have to keep it the same. You put your hands on your hips and keep them there."

"No, I move them up and then back down."

"No —"

Morgan interrupts. "You move them up at the end of the first line and then back down."

"Thanks, Morgan," Jordan beams, triumphant.

"Roll. Speed. Mark, action!" A long pause. Jordan shakes his head.

"I forgot my line," he confesses. "I'm thinking too much where my hands have to be."

September 30, 1995, Blair Field, Long Beach, California.

It is Jordan's last day on the set, a location shoot where the director will get some "pick-up shots" at the small baseball field. By noon, two hundred extras have been sitting in the bright sun for three hours. Jordan arrives at 1:30, his scheduled call. He has been out the night before with the departing basketball players. For the next few hours, the extras will crane for a glimpse of the star.

As part of the scene in which the baseball crowd sees a spaceship zoom up and over them, prop and effects personnel use a ball-launcher to fire a baseball over the bleachers at 160 mph. It creates a focal point for the extras to follow.

The extras are in a good mood, but grow tired as the sun gets hotter and hotter. While they wait for yet another camera setup, Jordan steps up to home plate with a bat and pops baseballs twenty feet up, then catches them with his gloved hand behind his back. The crowd cheers and Jordan smiles.

The scorching afternoon finally cools to evening. "Hey!" shouts Wayne Knight to Jordan. Knight is standing near the dugout and grabbing his crotch. "Am I doing a basketball player the right way?"

Once the live-action footage is finished, the material is then "photo-roto'ed," converting each frame to a black and white picture with holes punched so it fits an animator's pegboard. Now comes the long and patience-testing process of animation.

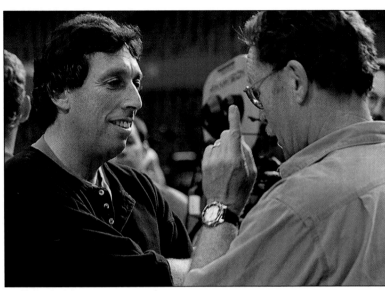

Cinematographer Michael Chapman consults Ivan Reitman about the composition of a shot.

Chicken wire

Listen, ah-say, listen up, son! If ya wanta make it big in pictures, ya gotta get up with the chickens! This here's movie life, not an oil paintin' (boy's so slow *molasses* gets bored with him)! Ya gotta move! Put some spring in y' giblets! Ya gotta be fast or you'll nevah get a break! Fast, break. Fast break! It's a joke, son! Make the team proud or find y'self a new jersey! New, jersey! New Jersey! I'm feedin' 'em to ya but you're fowlin' out, boy!

Michael Jordan has his forehead sponged between takes as Joe Pytka and his camera crew prepare for a shot.

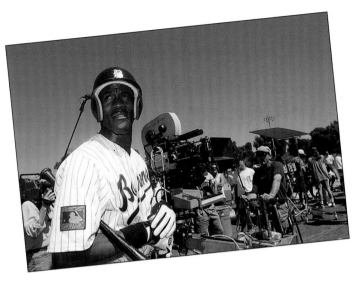

But I'm a baseball player now

Michael Jordan goes on location to Blair Field in Long Beach, California, which doubles as the stadium for the Birmingham Barons. Jordan shared some funny and occasionally absurd baseball experiences with the scriptwriters, who visited him in Birmingham. Some of the material ended up on the screen.

Ivan Reitman and Joe Pytka assess a camera angle as Bugs Bunny looks on.

Pytka and Jordan enjoy a relaxed moment while filming the movie's baseball sequences.

JOE HAS HIS OWN VISION OF WHAT HE WANTS HIS TEAM TO BE. HE'S MY LEADER... I TRUST HIS JUDGMENT.

— *Michael Jordan*

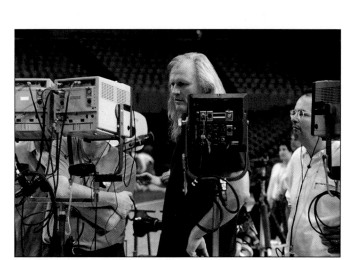

Joe Pytka and producer Danny Goldberg review action on a playback monitor.

"Joe Pytka, I thought, was the perfect man to direct this."

Ivan chose Joe Pytka based on the director's commercial work and his visceral style, as well as the fact that he'd worked with Michael Jordan before. "We'd seen a bunch of Michael's commercials," recalls Joe Medjuck, Reitman's longtime executive producer, "and virtually all of the ones we liked, Joe had directed."

Interview

Q & A: Joe Pytka

March 7, 1996. Pytka's offices, Venice, California. Joe Pytka, whose award-winning commercials have challenged the way images and motion are used to sell a spectrum of products, is every bit as tall as the basketball players he directs in *Space Jam*, and just as formidable. With shoulder-length white hair, a strong brow, and an (initially) gruff manner, Pytka seems more like a Norse warrior than a filmmaker.

Q: Did you have any reservations about approaching a project like *Space Jam?*

A: No.

Q: What was it like to do the first ever Looney Tunes feature?

A: The big challenge in terms of a [Looney Tunes] feature film is similar to a challenge you would face in any feature film — keeping the characters intact, making sure they do everything that is true to their character, without much deviation. So the biggest challenge has been to keep them in character and to give them a slightly fresher look. I've discovered the characters through the animators. We referred to what has been done in the past, but we've changed the way they are seen by the camera so that the dynamic will last over the whole length of a feature film.

Q: How do you mean "change the way they are seen by the camera"?

A: We are making the characters more dimensional; in other words, coming at you or [moving] away from you, coming up and down from all kinds of different perspectives. Before, everything used to play like this, very simply.

He holds up his hands to frame the air, and then moves his index finger from left to right.

Q: You're known for using a rather improvisational style in your work, instinctive . . .

A: Which drives people crazy sometimes.

Q: Do you go into it with a vision of what you want to do, or do you wait and try to read the moment?

A: It's a combination of both. I never liked working with storyboards unless we had to. We used the storyboards for live action so we knew what to do with Michael [in relation to the animation]. But you have to breathe life into something by waiting for a spontaneous, realistic moment and provide for that. I believe in a moment that's fresh and original and try to create from that moment. We did a lot of improvisation early on, stuff like that, and it worked out beautifully.

Q: Does that create problems?

A: It makes the editor's job a little more difficult sometimes. It makes the other camera people's jobs more difficult sometimes. But I believe firmly in trying to do stuff that is totally spontaneous.

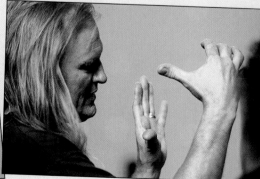

The hard work of moviemaking

Joe Pytka has a reputation for innovation and an absolute trust in his own instincts. Working with Ivan Reitman's creative team provided him with an award-winning means for carrying out his vision for *Space Jam*.

Chapman shares an idea with Pytka.

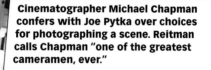

Cinematographer Michael Chapman confers with Joe Pytka over choices for photographing a scene. Reitman calls Chapman "one of the greatest cameramen, ever."

Joe Pytka, who has directed Michael Jordan in several projects, gives his star a description of the action in the scene they will be shooting. Pytka uses his hands with the same intensity that a symphony conductor uses a baton.

DOG-PILE ON THE DIRECTOR! DOG-PILE ON THE DIRECTOR!

Course work

The Arrowhead Country Club in Lake Arrowhead, California, becomes a golf course in Birmingham, Alabama, where Michael is grabbed by the Looney Tunes. There are no complaints about the long waits between shooting: Jordan, Knight, Bill Murray, and Larry Bird play a lot of real golf between takes.

Wayne Knight, as Stan, tears up the course trying to find Michael, who's been sucked into the cup. An isolated area of Los Angeles's Griffith Park does stand-in work, since Arrowhead would not allow for a divot this size.

Shawn Bradley chats with his fellow actors during a break in shooting.

On location in Los Angeles, Charles Barkley's character is beaten by a group of girls on a basketball court; as a last resort, he even swears off dating Madonna.

The theft of dapper Larry Johnson's playing skills sends him to a psychiatrist's couch.

The scene of Jordan's return to the gym for the players to recapture their talent has to be shot and reshot because the actors — Shawn Bradley, Patrick Ewing, Charles Barkley, Larry Johnson, and Muggsy Bogues — can't keep a straight face during a ceaseless barrage of ad libs.

Jordan holds the ball containing the powers of the five NBA stars. Later it will be made to glow through the use of special effects.

Interview

Ivan Reitman

November 14, 1995. Northern Lights offices, Universal City, California. Ivan Reitman is in a black sweatshirt and baggy pants. He is calm and direct, with probing eyes. Outside his office is a popcorn machine, giving the entire building the reassuring smell of a movie theater.

On Larry Johnson:

❝A menacing persona, but . . . very sweet and loving underneath. I also think that he has great natural acting instincts . . . unself-conscious. He was more comfortable with the filming process because he had done a lot of commercials.❞

On Muggsy Bogues:

❝I wanted him in the movie very much because I think it's a real inspiration for kids to see someone that small be so successful at a game of giants. He's also a wonderful personality. He shines.❞

On Bugs Bunny:

❝Bugs Bunny has always been my favorite animated character. He crosses generations of comedians, comedians I've loved. People like Bugs because he represents the kind of person we'd like to be: on top of it, wise, humorous, never in trouble, a protector of the weak, and a destroyer of the pretentious.❞

On Shawn Bradley:

❝[He was] the only one of all the players there who was truly interested in the filmmaking process. He sat behind the monitor whenever he could to see what was going on, and asked a lot of questions.❞

On Charles Barkley:

❝He's an intimidating force. He's got great, real comic skills. Probably could be an actor. I think you sense his energy and his power all the time.❞

On Patrick Ewing:

❝He's got this great big heart. Very sweet, very helpful to me. He's a natural captain and leader. People respect him. He's a real funny guy, too — this wonderful kind of Jamaican sort of [comical] sensibility. I've become a big fan of his as a result of the filming.❞

On Michael Jordan:

❝Beyond being a great basketball player . . . he could become a great actor if he wanted to. He's really remarkable for how well he is able to live with the pressures of unbelievable superstardom. He's very, very competitive — it's probably something in him [that] drove him as a very young man to do great things. That kind of drive sometimes brings down and destroys people. But it made him strive for excellence in the finest sort of way.❞

Family matters

Michael Jordan's role as a family man isn't a stretch for him. "Anything that he does that appeals to children, I always encourage. Anything that makes your children happy makes you happy," says Juanita Jordan, played here by Theresa Randle. "As a role model, what he does with Bugs Bunny and the characters is going to make children relate to him more."

Jordan developed a warm relationship with his on-screen children: Eric Gordon (below, who plays Michael's youngest son, Marcus), Penny Bae Bridges (bottom right, playing Jasmine Jordan and using her screen dad as a pillow), and Manner "Mooky" Washington (Jeffrey Jordan). Real-life daughter Jasmine gets a kiss as Penny looks on.

Juanita and Michael Jordan share a light moment together on the set. Marcus Jordan gets a ride while Jasmine Jordan studies her father's famous profile. Jordan's time with his children is precious, and he takes the moments whenever he can, as seen below with oldest son Jeffrey on the green screen stage.

Interview

The Two Mrs. Jordans

April 18, 1996. Juanita Jordan, from her home in Chicago. Juanita Vanoy Jordan met her husband in the late 1980s when she was a loan officer at a Chicago bank. She and Michael Jordan have three children. She's exceedingly gracious and thoughtful, with an easy laugh.

On Theresa Randle:
❝I was happy with the choice. We spoke briefly, but other than that, I just watched her. It was kind of strange seeing someone else playing the role of Michael's wife, but I thought she did a great job. ❞

On Her Kids and Bugs Bunny:
❝They believe in Bugs Bunny like the Easter Bunny and Santa Claus. If someone had come up to them dressed like Bugs Bunny on the set, they would've really thought that was Bugs. They were excited to know [Michael] was going to be with Bugs. They said, 'Oh, really?' Like now he's really cool. ❞

On Watching the Shoot:
❝Our kids wondered, *Why couldn't we play us?* and I told them no, they were too young, that this was really for the actors — the professional actors. They were able to watch the screen and listen on the headphones. When they heard their names they would just laugh and they thought that was really neat. They were glad to witness it all, but they still thought they could have done it themselves. ❞

On Her Husband's Acting Career:
❝This is certainly going to add more pressure to his life, but that doesn't bother him. I was really amazed, but I wasn't surprised. I knew the level of experience he had on [the commercial] level, but not on the level of making a movie: the long hours, the time on the set, having nothing to do. Just to be able to deal with that, and then get up when it's time for you to do your scene and remember your lines and perform — I was proud of him. ❞

March 14, 1996. Theresa Randle, at her publicist's office in Los Angeles. She starred in *Girl 6*, for which she was widely praised. Randle is young, beautiful, and pleasantly self-possessed, much like her idol, Bette Davis.

On Playing Juanita Jordan:
❝I really wanted to be true to the role. I'm thinking to myself, *I've got to talk to Juanita.* But Joe Pytka wanted me to play her as a character — the movie version. She came to the set one day, but they didn't want me to talk to her. I thought it would be a great thing to do, but they wanted me to play the public persona that I've seen and not to study her. It was very easy to play her as a loving wife. ❞

On Acting with Michael Jordan:
❝I think at first he was a little nervous, then he realized our energy [together] and the energy of the actors around him. As long as we were normal, he didn't have to fear anything. I tried to put him at ease and let him know that. Acting is just like playing basketball. It's fun. You have to enjoy it, otherwise there's no reason to do it. ❞

The Green Team

When Michael Jordan steps in front of the green screen on Soundstage 22 at Warner Bros., he is the only one who's not dressed in green. That's because, eventually, everything green will be matted out with a computer-generated image. The actors in the green outfits — in this scene playing the Monstars — will be animated over. They are living reference points for the actor and director. The red balls on the background are numbered, and provide a grid against which the special effects technicians can create a "virtual environment" of a gym, tracking the movement of the camera spatially in its relation to the balls. Film shot with Pytka's "wild camera" technique and Jordan's unpredictable moves wouldn't have been possible to merge with animation five years ago, but innovations in technology allow for the creation of a background that moves with the camera rather than having to program or "lock down" the camera's movement. So Pytka's lens and Jordan's moves retain their vigor and spontaneity while precisely interacting with the animation and background.

Special effects technology takes a huge hop forward

Michael Jordan uses a real basketball in *Space Jam,* but it isn't real all the time. Ed Jones, the Academy Award–winning visual effects supervisor *(Who Framed Roger Rabbit)* and designer of the proprietary effects software used in *Space Jam,* explains that the ball is real only when it's in Michael's possession. "Then the animators draw just the ball for whenever the [animated characters] have it, and I take that line drawing and turn it into a computer-generated basketball." Jones's CG basketball looks real, and is computer designed based on the real ball. When it leaves Jordan's hand, or when Bugs passes to him, it's a computerized ball until it reaches the exact frame in which it comes into Michael's possession. So Jordan can pass, catch, and steal at random from and to the animated characters. "The audience perceives it to be the same ball," Jones says. "You do not know the difference at all."

Jordan is spritzed (above) as the cameras prepare to roll. (right) While trying to establish an eyeline, a green screen actor breaks the star's composure with a wisecrack, after which Jordan focuses on playing to his yet-to-be-animated costars.

Michael prepares to tip the ball with Blanko, one of the Monstars. The actor who provides Jordan with an eyeline is standing on a small stool to achieve the height required for a Monstar.

Green screen actors playing Daffy, Taz, and Bugs join hands with Michael before the Ultimate Game.

Michael drives down the green screen court.

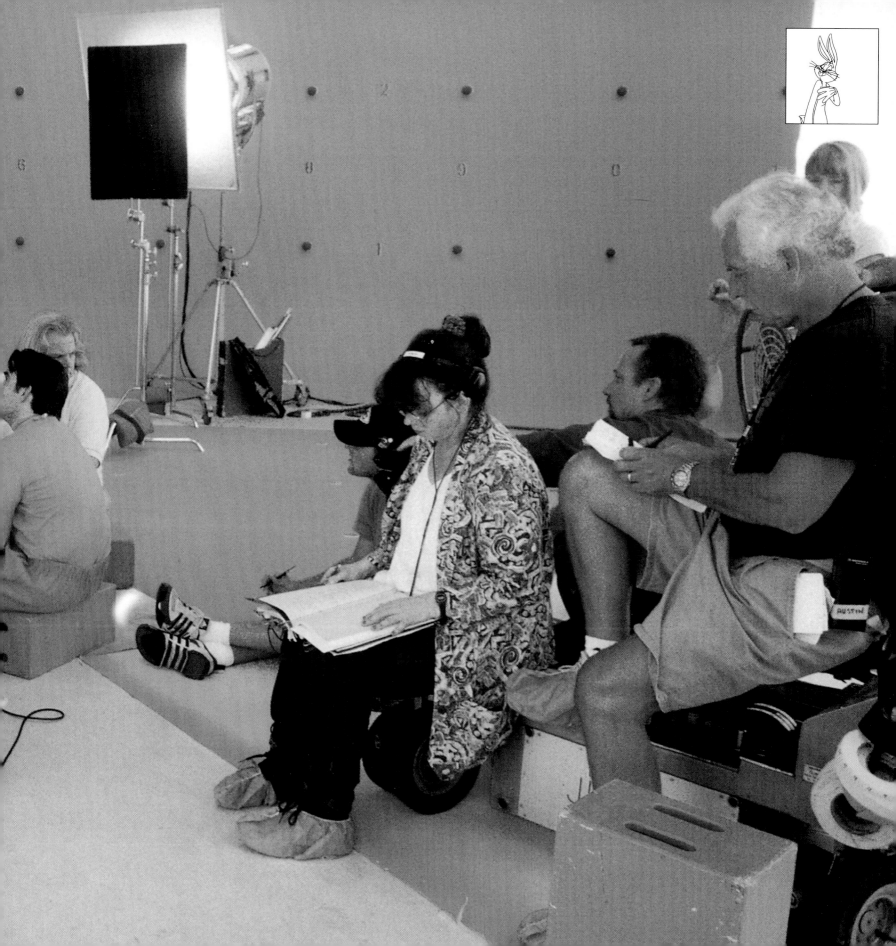

SHOOT ME NOW! SHOOT ME NOW!

As the camera rolls, Michael Jordan plays a heated, spontaneous game of basketball with the Monstars, who are represented by these green-suited players/actors.

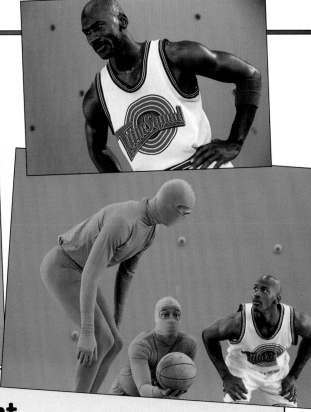

Interview

Q & A: Wayne Knight

September 25, 1995. John Marshall High School. People recognize Wayne Knight instantly, but they don't know from where. He's best known as the mercenary scientist in *Jurassic Park* and as the dorkish mailman on *Seinfeld*. In person, he's much more serious than his on-screen personas would lead one to expect.

Q: What's it been like working with Michael Jordan?

A: Once you get past that it's Michael Jordan, the legend himself, it's very easy. He works hard and he's pretty damned good as an actor.

Q: He seems to be a good listener.

A: He is, and he gets involved in every aspect of filmmaking. He wants to know who everyone is, and what everyone does. He listens to your lines and can get involved in them by reacting appropriately to the lines as it's called for.

Q: How do you play to animated costars?

A: I'm sort of used to working with characters who aren't all there. We didn't have any animatronic dinosaurs for *Jurassic Park* either, so we had to pretend these giant monsters were in front of us. It's important to create eye contact with the characters. I had to remind myself that I'm talking to little people. So I'm talking to the actors' knee caps and not looking into their eyes.

Q: Your part is very, very different from *Jurassic Park.* You're not as shrewd a guy in this one.

A: That's one of the reasons I'm really glad to be taking this nice-guy part, because kids all over the world think I'm an evil character. That's the kids. The adults usually want to talk to me about my role on *Seinfeld.*

Q: I hear they put some of the green screen actors on platforms to help you and Michael visualize the Monstars.

A: Yeah, as much as you can possibly visualize them. They also built these little rubber characters of each of the Looney Tunes, and that helped us place where we were talking, as far as Road Runner's beak or Tweety's eyes, or Yosemite Sam's face. I didn't know that varmint was so short, did you?

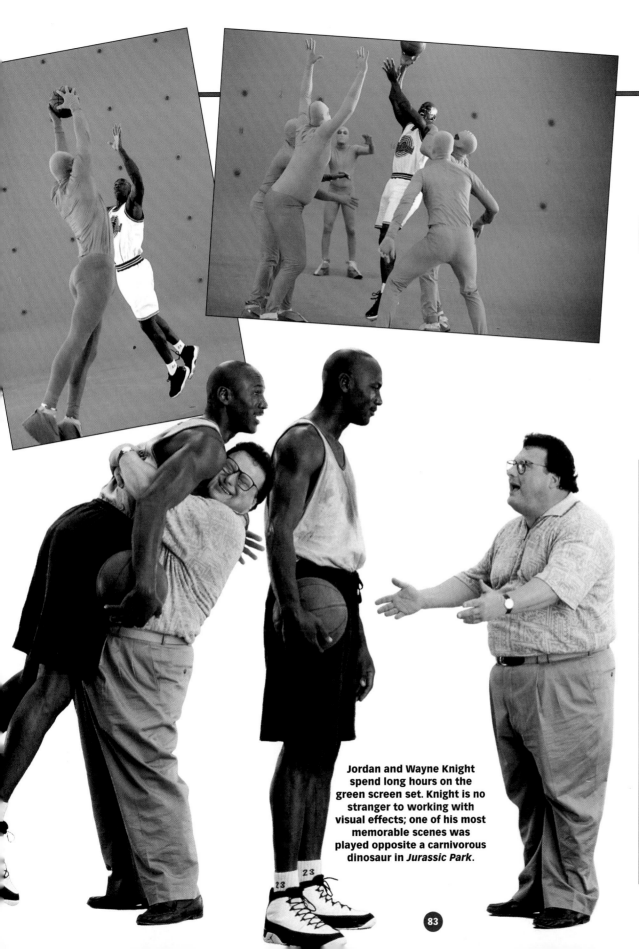

Jordan and Wayne Knight spend long hours on the green screen set. Knight is no stranger to working with visual effects; one of his most memorable scenes was played opposite a carnivorous dinosaur in *Jurassic Park*.

Interview

Q & A: Yosemite Sam

September 18, 1995. Warner Bros. Studios, Burbank. The sign on the door of the dressing room trailer says *Y. Sam*. Scotch-taped to the door is another sign, scrawled in crayon, that says *Git*. Yosemite Sam has always had a tenuous relationship with the press, with people, with reality in general. Today, though, his assistant assures everyone that the combustible star is eager to talk to them and pose for photos.

Q: Hello, Sam. Can I ask you a couple of questions about *Space Jam* and working with Michael Jordan and Bugs Bunny?

A: NO!! K — N — O!

Q: Thank you for your time.

Court gestures

While Joe Pytka directs, Ivan Reitman has a chance to play and interact with the NBA players. For the scenes in which the NBA stars lose their powers, Reitman stocked the L.A. Sports Arena with a roster of the best players ever to step on a court. Most of them were eager to participate because of Michael Jordan's friendship and integrity, despite the on-court rivalry between Jordan and many of the stars present.

Reitman gleefully explains to the team players their parts in the storyline of the film.

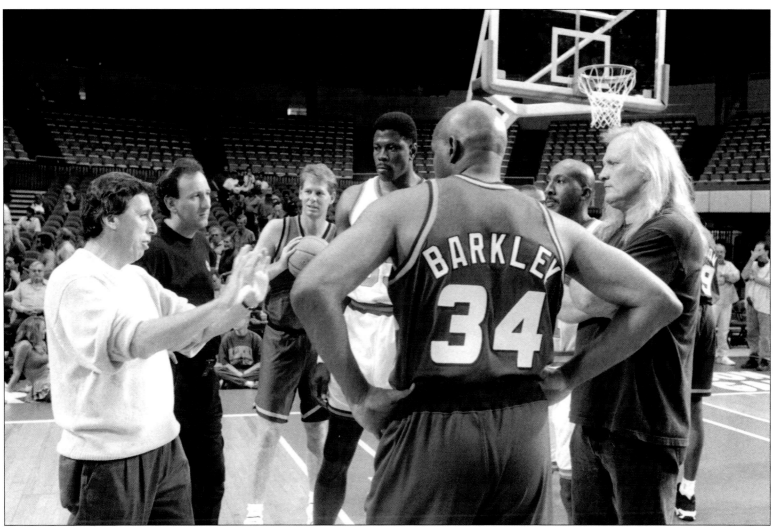

Ivan Reitman, Ken Ross, and Joe Pytka discuss the execution of a scene as Patrick Ewing, Charles Barkley, Danny Ainge, and Derek Harper listen.

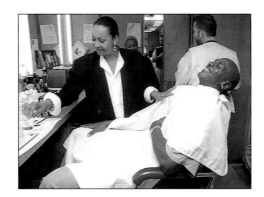

I'D A' BEEN THERE, BUT I WAS GETTIN' A FACIAL.

— *Bugs Bunny*

The stars come out

Great basketball players, like great comic actors, are heroes of instinct, intuition, and energy. Despite the long periods of waiting on the set, they listened, they focused, and they performed. "They're entertainers, after all," says Joe Pytka. "We drew upon their powers and they were very giving of their sense of humor about themselves. We made fun of them for what they do, and they all did willingly play."

Joe Pytka is about to conduct a shot with a "team" portraying the Charlotte Hornets.

Production manager Gordon Webb poses with Derek Harper and Patrick Ewing.

Action! Charles Barkley uses his powers to play like he's losing his powers.

(Far left) Michael Jordan borrows Michael Chapman's chair to view the composition of a shot as Joe Pytka looks on.

Set Pieces

Despite the frantic pace, the temperature, and the lag time, everyone had a favorite moment from the shoot.

66 The most fun I had was on the day that Hideo Nomo came on the set and shook hands with Michael Jordan. I felt like I was among royalty. 99
— *Wayne Knight*

66 The day we were with the players at the Sports Arena. It's a real basketball fan's dream. 99
— *Ivan Reitman*

66 I think just hanging around the locker room telling jokes about Michael, since he wasn't there to defend himself. 99
— *Pooh Richardson*

66 The funniest thing was looking up at that scoreboard and seeing that they had the Knicks scoring 79 points at the beginning of the fourth quarter. We're still laughing about that — definitely make-believe. 99
— *A. C. Green*

66 I like renewing some of my old acquaintances. I like being around basketball again. We've been trading around old basketball stories, talking about who's the best player in the NBA and who some of the new guys are in the profession. 99
— *Marques Johnson*

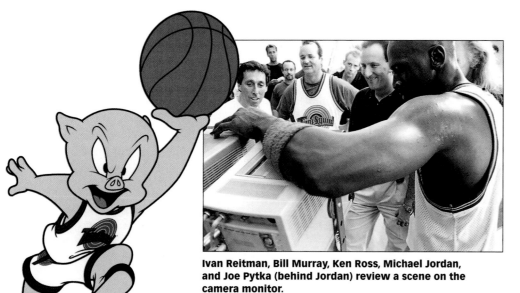

Ivan Reitman, Bill Murray, Ken Ross, Michael Jordan, and Joe Pytka (behind Jordan) review a scene on the camera monitor.

Call-waiting

A call sheet chronicles the events of the upcoming day in a live-action shoot, designating who should be where, and when. Call sheets are an essential organizational tool in moviemaking, giving the production crew specific information about the day's goals. It also describes the scenes to be shot, special equipment needed, props, even the animals hired.

> I WAS GOING TO BE THE LEAD MONSTAR WHO WASN'T AS TALL AS THE OTHERS. I REHEARSED FOR NOTHING. NOW I'M A DUCK.

— *Steve Kehela,*
Groundling member,
green screen actor,
and Daffy stand-in

Jordan, Reitman, Ross, and Murray confer before shooting a scene, while (below) green screen actors rehearse with Murray and Jordan.

"SPACE JAM"

REVISED

Production # 135184
Warner Bros/ Northern Lights
100 Universal City Plaza
Universal City, 91608

PO# J0200Z

Sunrise: 6:22A Sunset: 7:27P
Weather:

DAY 30 OF 60   Mon, 09/11/95

CREW CALL: 730A
SHOOT CALL: 9A

Producers: I. Reitman/ J. Medjuck/ D. Goldberg
Exec Prod: K. Ross, D. Falk
Co Producer: G. Webb
Director: J. Pytka

No Forced Calls w/o UPM/ AD Approval

NOTE: CLOSED SET, NO VISITORS W/OUT PERMISSION FROM THE PRODUCTION OFFICE.
ALL CREW MEMBERS ARE REQUIRED TO WEAR WARNER BROS SECURITY BADGES.

SET	SCENES	CAST	PAGE	D/N	LOCATION
TO BEGIN: (ORDER MAY CHANGE)					Stage 12/1
INT. MICHAEL'S HOUSE - TROPHY ROOM					Warner Bros
* Jasmine sees Tunes steal shorts, Charles guards	103	6,61,63,Dog	0-4/8	N8	Burbank
* Bugs & Daffy try to distract Charles - PLATE	103B	4,5,6,61,63, Dog	0-1/8	N8	
* Kids peek, hide	104	61,63	0-2/8	N8	
* Marcus calls Charles, gives Bugs shorts	107	4,5,6,61,63, Dog	1-0/8	N8	
INT. MICHAEL'S HOUSE - BOYS' ROOM					
* Jasmine says "There's cartoons"	103A	4,5,6	0-1/8	N8	
INT. MICHAEL'S HOUSE - JASMINE'S ROOM					
* Jasmine wakes, sees shadows	98E	6	0-1/8	N8	
EXT. MICHAEL'S HOUSE - FRONT DOOR					
* Bugs opens door to Daffy	98C	61,63	0-2/8	N8	
INT. MICHAEL'S HOUSE - HALLWAY					
* Daffy & Bugs go down hallway - PLATE	98D	nada	0-1/8	N8	Crew Park
INT. CHARLES' DOG HOUSE					USUAL STA
* Daffy & Charles come face to face	98A	63, Dog	0-1/8	N8	PARKING ST

TECH SCOUT @ WRAP: J. PYTKA, D. GOLDBERG, B. WILSON, A. McCANN, M. CHAPMAN
J. KOUZOUYAN, B. PROCHAL, S. WILLIAMS, B. SCHINDLER, G. KIRKLAND,
J. WILLIAMS, J. LIMA, P. EASLEY, E. JONES, B. KOCH, D. JOHNSON

CAST	PART OF	STATUS	MU/HAIR	SET CALL	REMARKS
1. Michael Jordan	Michael Jordan	H			
2. Wayne Knight	Stan Podolak	H			
4. Manner Washington (k)	Jeffrey Jordan (10)	SW	930A	11A	
5. Eric Gordon (k)	Marcus Jordan (6-1/2)	SW	1030A	11A	
6. Penny Bae Bridges (k)	Jasmine Jordan (5)	SW	1230P	1P	
90. Nate Bellamy	Stunts	H			

ANIMATED CAST	PART OF	STATUS	CALL TIME	SET CALL	REMARKS
61. John Crane	Bugs	W	8A	8A	(off camera only)
62. Frederica Kesten	Various	W	8A	8A	(off camera only)
63. Steve Kehela	Daffy	H			
64. John Ducey	Various	H			
65. Jim Wise	Various	H			
66. June Melby	Various	H			

STANDINS	Rpt @	ATMOSPHERE		Rpt @	Instructions
3 Standins (Penny,Eric,Manner)	7A	1 "Jasmine" Double (k)		1030A	Report to Crew Parking
					NDB on all Background

SPECIAL INSTRUCTIONS

PROPS:	Bugs & Daffy Macquettes. Michael's gym bag, Sox, Shoes, NC gym shorts	
ART/SETS:	Basketball memorabilia, Door on floor (Trophy Room) Match outside door to location (Sc 98C)	
WARDROBE:	NC gym shorts & doubles	
PRODUCTION:	Closet door off (Sc 103pt)	

SPECIAL INSTRUCTIONS

CAMERA:	Hot head
GRIP:	Leni Arm, Louma Crane (Sc 98E)
SPFX:	Sox, shoes into bag, Stuff moves. Door c Doors open & close (Trophy Room) Car up, Door opens (Front Door)
VFX:	Animators on board
ANIMALS:	Charles snarls, w/ shorts in mouth, Door approaches, ignores stuff, releases sho

ADVANCE SCHEDULE

DAY/DATE	SET	SCENE #	CAST	PAGES	LOCATI
Tues, 09/12/95 & Wed, 09/13/95 DAY #31 & DAY #32	Int. Michl's Hse - Trophy Rm (N8) Int. Jasmine's Room (N8)	103,103A.103B,104,107, 98E	4,5,6,61,63	1-6/8	Stage 1
Thurs, 09/14/95 DAY #33	Int. Greenscreen (E9)	126pt,135pt,152pt,153pt	2,Tunes,Stars	1-3/8	Stage 2
Fri, 09/15/95 DAY #34	Int. Greenscreen (?)	TBD	TBD		Stage 2
Mon, 09/18/95 DAY #35	Int. Seance Room (DX3) Int. Psychiatrist's Office (D9)	95E 121pt	26,27,28,29,48 26,27,28,51	0-6/8 1-3/8	Stage
Tues, 09/19/95 DAY #36	Int. Hospital Corridor (D8)	95	26,27,28,29,44, 55	0-7/8	CIGNA
	Int. Medical Clinic Office (DX2)	95D	26,27,28,29	0-1/8	
	Int. Medical Office (DX4)	95F	26,27,28,29,49	0-5/8	
	Int. Doctor's Office (DX1)	95C	28,47	0-3/8	

1st AD: _(signature)_ A. McCann
2nd AD: Pamela Cederquist
UPM: _(signature)_ Gordon W

WARNER BROS.

CALL SHEET

"SPACE JAM" PO#

PRODUCTION #135184   CREW CALL: 730A

REVISED

DATE: MONDAY, 09/11/95

Production		Time
Director:	J. PYTKA	730A
Prod Mgr	G. WEBB	O/C
2U 1st AD:	B. WILSON	O/C
1st A.D.:	A. McCANN	730A
Key 2nd AD:	P. CEDERQUIST	7A
2nd 2nd AD:	B. HEBERT	542A
2U 2nd AD:	M. NEWMAN	O/C
DGA Trainee:	W. KILLIAN	9A
Key Staff:	J. TABACK	730A
Staff Asst:	J. WEBB	7A
Staff Asst:		
Script Super:	J. SAUNDERS	730A
Script Super:	MORGAN	730A
Teacher:	TBD	730A
Dialg Coach:	TK CARTER	930A
B-ball Coord:	N. MIGUEL	O/C

Camera		Time
Dir.of Photog:	M. CHAPMAN	7A
Camera Op:	B. ROE	730A
1st Asst Cam	J. BARBER	712A
2nd Asst Cam	J.LaFARGO	712A
Loader:	J. MILLER	712A
Camera Op:	F. PERL	
1st Asst Cam	S. ADCOCK	
2nd Asst Cam	S. WAGNER	
Camera Op:	D. LUCKNBACH	
1st Asst Cam	J. THIBO	
2nd Asst Cam	TBD	
Still Photog:	B. TALAMON	730A
Camera:	STEDICAM	ON TRUCK
Camera:	PANAVISION	ON TRUCK
Equipment	POWER POD	ON TRUCK

Video		Time
Vid Asst:	R. SPERRY	730A
Staff Asst:		

Electric		Time
Gaffer:	J. KOUZOUYAN	6A
Best Boy:	TBD	6A
WB Best Boy:	S. FIELDSTEEL	542A
Lamp Op:	T. MORRIS	6A
Lamp Op:	D. WINDELS	6A
Lamp Op:	C. BIBB	6A
Lamp Op:	F. IRVING	6A
Lamp Op:	G. KITTLESON	6A
Lamp Op:		
Lamp Op:		
Rigging:	B. PROCHAL+2	
Local 40:	POWERHOUSE	542A

Grip		Time
Key Grip:	S. WILLIAMS	6A
Best Boy:	G. BORTHWICK	6A
Best Boy:	S. STRAUSER	6A
WB Best Boy:	T. CONLEY	6A
Dolly Grip:	D. BUTKOVICH	6A
Dolly Grip:	M. FLETCHER	6A
Co Grip:	B. SCHINDLER	6A
Co Grip:	T. JOHNSON	6A
Co Grip:	P. WILKOWSKY	6A
Co Grip:	B. SANTUCCI	6A
Co Grip:		
Co Grip:		
Dolly	FISHER #10	ON TRUCK
Crane	LENI ARM	ON TRUCK

Sound		Time
Mixer:	R. JOHNSON	730A
Boom:	M. CHMBRLAIN	730A
Cable:	M. JENNINGS	730A
35 Walkie-Talkies		ON TRUCK

Studio Personnel		Time
Local 40:	Max for AC	7A
Local 40:		
Flag Men		
Security:	SANDRA/KEITH	8A
Security:	Jordan Dome	24hrs
Fire Safety:		

Wardrobe		Time
Supervisor:	C. LAWRENCE	O/C
Set Costumer:	Y. BRADDY	9A
Set Costumer:	E HANLEY	O/C
Set Costumer:	G. REILLY	O/C
Set Costumer:	BJ ROGERS	O/C
Addl Costumer:		

Make-Up/Hair		Time
Key Makeup:	C. REECE-THORNE	912A
Addl Makeup:	L. THOMPSON	
Body Makeup:		
Key Hair:	L. WAGGONER	912A
Hairstylist:	M. HART	
Addl Hair:		

Props		Time
Propmaster:	S. MANNION	730A
Asst Prp Mstr:	J. SEXSMITH	730A
Addl Props:		
Trainer:	K. McELHATTON	730A
Animal:	"CHARLES"	730A

Special Effects		Time
Coordinator:	D. PRITCHETT	730A
Foreman:	K. CLARK	O/C
Staff Asst:	A. SEABOK	O/C
Staff Asst:	RC PRITCHETT	O/C
Staff Asst	J. GUARERRA	O/C

Small Crafts		Time
CSE:	D.HECKLER	
1st Aid:		7A
S/B Painter:	R. PUGA	730A

Production Office		Time
Secretary:	AF FENADY	O/C
Asst Sectry:	R. VAUPEL	O/C
Staff Asst:	A. SCARANO	O/C
Staff Asst:	A. HOLZENDORF	O/C
Staff Asst:	U. LVLYCOLORS	O/C
Staff Asst:	J. CHINICH	O/C
Staff Asst:	P. VOGEL	O/C
Publicist:	M. BATTAGLIA	O/C

Accounting		Time
Accountant:	S. BOKOBZA	O/C
Asst Acctant:	S. BOKOBZA	O/C
2nd Asst Acct:	EG ALVARADO	O/C
Payroll Asst:	S. BUTENSKY	O/C
Cnstrctn Aud:	K. ANDERSON	O/C

Art Department		Time
Prod. Designer:	G. KIRKLAND	O/C
Art Director:	D. KLASSEN	O/C
Sr Ld Set Des:	D. WIGHT	O/C
Set Designer:	M. RUBEO	O/C
Researcher:	A. BURNHAM	O/C
Staff Asst:	M. BLACK	O/C

Set Dressing		Time
Set Decorator:	J. WILLIAMS	O/C
Lead Person:	S. HULL	O/C
Swing Gang:	M. HANRAHAN	O/C
Swing Gang:	P. FORD	O/C
Swing Gang:	M. BOUCHER	O/C
Swing Gang:	D. PILLER	O/C
On Set:	M. BROWN	730A

Stage		Time
Open Stage	Stage 12/18	630A
Air Conditng	Stage 12/18	630A
Heat	Stage	
Red Light	Stage 12/18	XXXX
Security	Stage 12/18	XXXX
Wig-Wags	Stage 12/18	XXXX
3 Drssg Rms	Stage 12/18	XXXX
Blowers	Stage 12/18	7A

Catering		Time
Breakfasts	Ready @	
Lunches	Ready @	
Soup		
Extras Chairs		
Addl Helper:		
2nd Line:		

Locations		Time
Loc'n Mgr:	I. ROSENSTEIN	O/C
Loc'n Liaison	V. ROBERT	O/C
Police:		per Loc
Security:		per Loc
FSO		per Loc
Locatn Liaison		per Loc

Construction		Time
Coordinator:	G. STOKES	O/C
Foreman:	J. ORENDORFF	O/C
Labor Frmn:	J. WARD	O/C
Labor Frmn:	T. BYRD	O/C
Paint Frmn:	R. PUGA	O/C
Greensman:	PD HARRIS	O/C
Greensman:	E. HARRIS	O/C

Editorial		Time
Editor:	S. KAHN	O/C
1st Asst:	R-CLAIRE	O/C
Apprentice:	D. PADGETT	O/C

Transportation		Time
Coordinator:	D. JOHNSON	O/C
Captain:	L. RODRIGUEZ	O/C
Drivers:	7	per DJ
Equipment:		
Camera 5-Ton		P
Electric 10-Ton		E
Grip 5-Ton		R
Prop Semi		
EFX Semi		T
Wrdrb Semi		R
Makeup Trailer		A
Cast Trailers (4)		N
Crew Cab	J. EL HABIB	S
Crew Cab	G. HRIVNAK	P
Crewcab	T. MacDONALD	O
Crewcab	B. McCANCE	R
Topkick	A. MOORE	T
Maxivan #1	J. BALDWIN	A
Maxivan #2	T. DRAGNA	T
Maxivan #3		I
Honeywagon		O
Tow Generators (2)		N
Picture Cars		

Animation		Time
Producer:	S. LEIVA	O/C
Prod/Dir:	J. REES	730A
Line Prod:	R. SULLIVAN	O/C
Prod Mgr:	L. HOUGH	O/C
Director:	R. ARONS	O/C
Director:	D. BAER	O/C
Director:	N. BOYLE	O/C
Director:	J. KAMMERUD	O/C
Director:	U. MEYER	O/C
Director:	B. SMITH	730A
Liaison:	C. CLEAVER	730A

Visual Effects		Time
Supervisor:	J. LIMA	730A
Prod Super:	P. EASLEY	730A
VFX Prod:	E. JONES	730A
Storyboard:	S. LABBY	O/C
Plate Coord:	B. KOCH	730A
Staff Asst:	M. PEREZ	O/C

HOSPITAL:

REVISED

MILEAGE:

Thermal layers

A thermal is a Polaroid-style photograph of the image on a camera's monitor. Thermals play a huge part in the filming process because they allow animators, standing by on the set, to sketch in backgrounds and characters that will be added in later stages of the production. The thermals give the live-action director a tangible view of his material in relation to what is on the storyboard panel. They show how the real Michael Jordan will look in a background that literally has to be created later by the animation and visual effects team. Rather than operate purely on faith, the director is given assurance that the scenes will look just as they were envisioned.

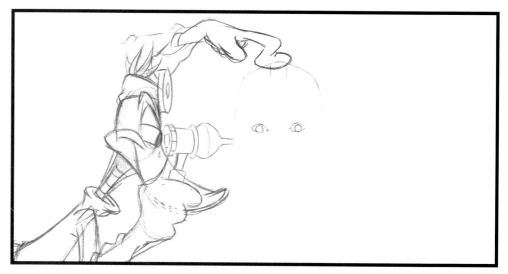

(top right) After Michael lands in Looney Tune Land, his ear is subject to inspection by Daffy, played by green screen actor Steve Kehela. (middle) The thermal image is pulled and Michael's face is set against a storyboard panel. Now the animator draws Daffy peering into Michael's ear. (bottom) This is the cleaned up animation art that was created for the film.

That's a wrap!

On the last day of the film's principal photography shoot, Michael Jordan is tired but in high spirits, bidding farewell to the cameramen and his costars. Balancing two high-scrutiny careers would be enough to wither most people, but Jordan handles it with a quiet modesty. As Jordan signs out to abundant praise for his movie work, he faces eight of the most strenuous (and highly scrutinized) months in his professional basketball career.

The camera captures Michael Jordan's strength and athleticism — through his legs.

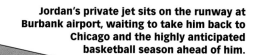

Leaving his dressing trailer, Michael Jordan signs out at the end of the last day of filming.

Jordan's private jet sits on the runway at Burbank airport, waiting to take him back to Chicago and the highly anticipated basketball season ahead of him.

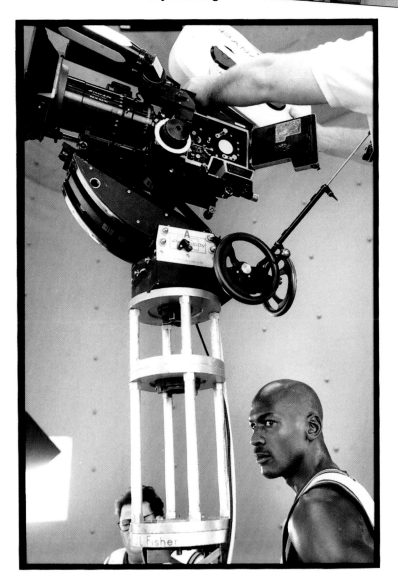

(above) Jordan stretches out in his jet just before takeoff, another precious moment of solitude away from the public Michael Jordan — a man known for being unafraid of challenges. His first venture into movies, under the intense scrutiny of a new set of cameras, seems only to reaffirm his eagerness to follow another new path to see where it would lead him.

3

DOME AWAY FROM HOME

It seemed to appear out of nowhere on the
Warner Bros. backlot — a basketball big top for members only
(and a few lucky visitors), where the stars came out at night
for a little five-on-five with the champ.

Uptime

A door slams loudly. Shouts. The erratic tom-tom of a basketball on a wooden court. Shoes squeal, pivot, turn. The floor shakes under the weight of ten supersized men charging, checking, pressing against each other for possession of the ball. A distinct smell of sweat, damp towels, and new carpet. A full court drive and four men are under the net. A turn for a shot. Gleaming, muscled arms reach, grab, twist at impossible angles for the block. A desperate launch. The hoop rattles angrily. Up for the rebound, for the shot again, blocked, the men's grunts and yells betraying the apparent grace of their movement. Bang! against the backboard, then the swish of a net. More shouts. Laughter. A hundred or so guests watch in awe. Applause. Tom-tom. A single bounce and the ball is again in play.

This is no pick-up game. This is nighttime, stops-out, off-season NBA basketball, right on the backlot of Warner Bros. Studios. This is Valhalla, Hollywood style. This is the Jordan Dome.

It seemed to materialize from nowhere. One minute there was an employee parking lot, then a huge wooden platform, like a barn floor, a mammoth edifice of white canvas. It was a curiosity, even at a movie studio, where unusual sets are built in the morning and gone by sundown.

Something as elaborate (and costly) as the Dome is an unusual

accommodation for a star, especially for his first movie. But Michael Jordan is, in all areas, uncommon. The Jordan Dome was partly a good-faith gesture by Warner Bros., an acknowledgment of the world's most famous athlete's uncompromising priorities. Jordan, who trains year-round, has always woven a strict physical regimen into his daily life. To snag the star for *Space Jam*, Warner Bros. had to create a convenient place for him to maintain his training

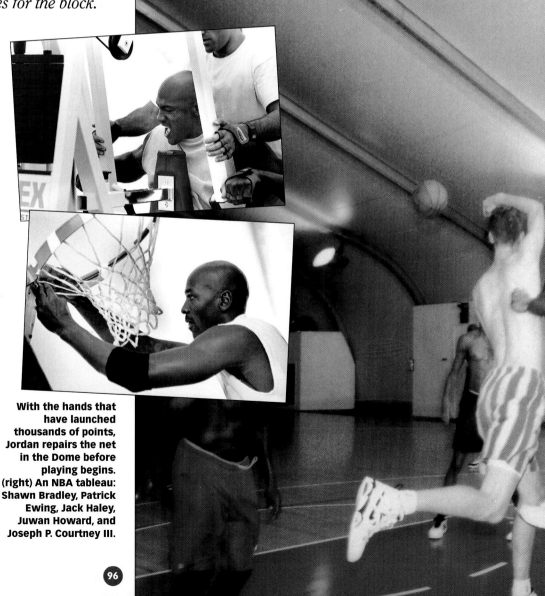

With the hands that have launched thousands of points, Jordan repairs the net in the Dome before playing begins. (right) An NBA tableau: Shawn Bradley, Patrick Ewing, Jack Haley, Juwan Howard, and Joseph P. Courtney III.

without taking him too far from the set. At the same time, the studio had to find time in Jordan's already overburdened schedule to shoot the film while he prepared for a personally crucial basketball season. The Dome became far more than its designers could have expected.

Both the studio and Ivan Reitman's production company asked Tim Grover, Jordan's personal trainer, to make a "wish list" for the facility. Grover held back nothing, expecting

that there would be cutbacks and trimming. "I requested specialized Cybex equipment related to basketball. We requested an NBA basketball floor with professional goals [hoops and backboards]. I needed an area for Mike to relax, a stereo system, a telephone, a fax machine [for business], a bathroom, and a towel and shower facility for everybody.

"I just took the blueprints of how I train him in Chicago and that's what we did out here. I made it [a place] where Michael and his guys and the other players could come and kick back and relax also."

For five days, a construction team built a huge foundation on top of the parking lot, taking special care in placing the basketball floor, which was rented from California State University, Long Beach, and delivered in sections. The superstructure, a twenty-eight-foot-high free-span aluminum frame, was then erected, and covered with thousands of square feet of white canvas stretched tightly over eleven tremendous support ribs. The air conditioning system was so powerful that, according to the construction supervisor, "you could hang meat in there." The facility was ready for play in little more than a week. "Everything I had requested was in there. Everything. It was beautiful," Grover recalls.

The Dome was an investment in expedience and convenience for everyone involved in the movie. "It's a selfish thing in certain ways," admits producer Dan Goldberg, who with Joe Medjuck has been Ivan Reitman's partner for years. "We *had* to make the

Jordan Dome. We wanted him close by so we could get him here quickly and not waste a lot of time, and we didn't want him lost in traffic or that sort of thing. He couldn't move his schedule. He really did have to play basketball, and he really did have to go and rehearse."

Jordan speaks to few people in the Dome, and has no interest in an interview. This is his life, basketball, and he throws himself into living it, and he has no need to stop along the way and answer questions about it. Not here. Another day, another topic, perhaps. Under the cathedral-like ceiling of the Dome, the subject for now is basketball, and there's no discussion necessary. It's alive, and it will not hold still long enough to comment on itself. This is full-out, sweat-and-sinew competition, and the stakes, for the moment, feel like all-out war.

The Dome was a place for the movie's athletes to shake out the frustration of the start-stop-wait pace of moviemaking, a place for a little uptime to make up for the hours of downtime. It was a place for athletes to be athletes again, testing one another's skills in a professional setting. It was never designed for amateurs, or an audience. At the Dome, Jordan could be among his equals. It was a safe place to set his stardom aside for awhile and play freely and unselfconsciously.

But everyone involved was slightly naive about the kind of interest a place like this would generate. Word quickly spread throughout the lot. Anticipation over the star's presence grew beyond anything Grover or Jordan could have guessed. Soon, solicitations to visit the Dome during workouts became a daily, then hourly, drain on Grover's time.

Naturally, Jordan's *Space Jam* costars were there (although because of injuries, some stayed off the court), a lineup of basketball luminaries that included Dennis

Jordan has a few moments of reflection— a luxury— before beginning his regular early morning workout.

Rodman (before his trade to the Bulls), Reggie Miller, Chris Mills, Alonzo Mourning, Shaquille O'Neal, Marques Johnson, Cedric Ceballos, Juwan Howard, Glenn Rice, Grant Hill, Rod Strickland, and — for the final day — Magic Johnson. The overwhelming response required Grover to schedule the number of players per night to accommodate everyone possible and create teams.

Magic Johnson arrived at the Dome on the last day of its use. He and Jordan hit the boards hard and fast, an intense but respectful competition that carried over to the 1995–96 season.

"The whole idea [at first] was to keep it closed to the public. But we had so many requests from people who worked for Warner Bros. — CEOs and so forth — that it wasn't possible to do that." Grover was forced to be trainer and diplomat. He rescheduled the day to give Jordan some time alone in the facility to meet his daily individual workout requirements. Grover opened things up to some of the studio staff and certain friends and families of the players after 7:00 P.M., when the evening basketball game began. The Dome became a pilgrimage site for anyone on the studio backlot, although most people were still not allowed inside without a personal invitation.

"When he's working out by himself, he doesn't want to be bothered," Grover explains. "We do some things that I don't see other [trainers and athletes] doing, and it's strictly for Michael that I've developed these exercises. He just turns on the music and we turn off all the phones and TVs. There is very little communication even between him and me. He's focused in on what he has to do."

The floor was mopped and waxed yesterday, and there's a sweet residual aroma of cleaner. Shirts and Skins. Half a dozen different basketball shoe brands and a stockbroker's weight in million-dollar contracts on one court. Focus. No cameras. No reporters. No mercy. No one here is going to go easy on Michael Jordan, and he's elevated by the challenge.

Jordan, for Skins, dribbles downcourt, blows past Juwan Howard, stops, covered by Reggie Miller, dips and sways to one side, dribbling the ball slowly at arm's length. He transfers the ball

to the other hand, spins, breaks away, takes four strides closer to the hoop, zigs to the right, dodges Chris Mills, shoots. The whole process takes maybe five seconds. The ball misses. Jordan's face flashes a moment of irritation, but his entire success is based on drive fueled by frustration.

Because of the usual frenzy in the wake of Jordan's celebrity, the Dome was assigned a twenty-four-hour security staff, and special badges were required. When guests were admitted for the evening's events, the list was limited to VIPs and a few lucky additions. "Michael is a star of stars. It's funny how he affects people," Grover says. "Stars want to meet Michael. He's that big. So I guess they knew he was in town and they just wanted to come by and say hello."

Schwarzenegger was there, and so was Antonio Banderas. Steven Seagal stopped in to watch. The cast of *Sisters*, shooting exteriors on the adjacent Midwest street set, was granted admission, as were the casts of *Friends* and *ER*. Although *ER* is set in Chicago, and basketball figures intermittently in the show (Jordan teammate Scottie Pippen filmed a cameo appearance on *ER* a few weeks later), none of the show's stars made any attempt to get on the court.

Of course, the Dome was open to any NBA player, which became especially timely because of the lockout in effect at the time. "With the NBA strike, all the summer leagues and all the practice facilities were closed," Grover says. "If you wanted to play the best basketball during the summer, this was the place to be." Grover contacted player agents and extended an open invitation to their clients. Soon, invitations became unnecessary.

"I would rank each player [on skill], and he would get the first opportunity to play. We would establish three teams with five players each. If you came in after that, it was too late. I had to formulate the best teams to get Michael back in shape and get his skills back to where they were." Despite Jordan's periodic absence for other obligations, Grover continued to open the Dome for players.

Dennis Rodman played, apparently to test the waters between Jordan and him before the trade. Their chemistry was judged successful, even inspiring.

Some nonprofessionals were allowed to play, but only after the pros had had their time on the court and were ready to step out. "I was very honored that they let me out there," admits Dean Cain, who plays Superman in the Warner Bros. television production *Lois and Clark*. Cain, a college football star, knew that he was taking his chances on the court with the no-nonsense NBA stars. "I know when to get out of the way when you're going to get slam-dunked on, and I did, especially with Michael."

Without the presence of the fabled and the mighty, the incongruous tent on the backlot could've been any basketball court. But for a few weeks during a particularly hot summer, the Jordan Dome was ground zero for the most explosive basketball in the world, played purely for the sport of it. To those left to covet the scarce sideline seats, it was a historical site where important things would happen, a place that would be gone all too soon. This was where the stars came out, away from the scrutiny of cameras and (most) fans and the press. Joe Pytka was a bit more grounded in his appraisal.

"They just came up there to play ball. It was a hangout. You were there. There was good music and everybody was up there playing. Where else are you going to go? If you want to play some ball, are you going to go to the Y or go to the Dome?"

No mercy

The Jordan Dome was no playground. *Space Jam* was filming during training time for the new season, and the players made the most of the facility. The play here was professional level, and if you were on the court, you were open game. The Dome became the place for the pros to hang out at night, doing what they do best *with* the best.

(top) Jordan defends himself against Juwan Howard, Reggie Theus, and LaSalle Thompson, then makes a drive (bottom) past Reggie Miller and Howard.

(left) With Jordan blocking, Shawn Bradley tries to assist Cedric Ceballos. (far left) Jordan eludes Cameron Dollar, Reggie Miller, and Cedric Ceballos.

Hang time: A lineup of the NBA's brightest stars waits for gravity to kick in.

With his personal trainer standing by, Jordan continues his rigorous training schedule, with stretching and cardio-vascular exercises in the morning, weight lifting at lunchtime, and, after a day of filming, a couple of hours of stops-out basketball at night.

Interview

Q & A: Tim Grover

March 7, 1996. Chicago. Tim Grover has just returned to his A.T.T.A.C.K. Athletics facility after taking Michael Jordan through his regular morning workout at Jordan's home.

Q: What were the ground rules for visitors at the Dome?

A: No autographs. No pictures. You can't bother the players. And please stay off the equipment. And don't expect to play. A lot of people thought, *Oh, it's a pick-up game,* but it wasn't that at all. We must have had $500 million worth of contracts and bodies in that gym at any time. We couldn't afford to have anybody get hurt.

Q: Was Michael's training pretty typical for an NBA player?

A: It was a lot more rigorous. Very few individuals have this kind of training program. But again, you're looking at a man who went eighteen months training for baseball and now wanted to get back into basketball, so a lot of extra work was needed.

Q: What's the most important aspect of a professional athlete's workout program?

A: Different things. You have eye/hand coordination, speed, explosiveness. You have to work on a little bit of everything. I don't care how effective a player is, if he has a weak link and keeps reinjuring himself, he's no good to himself or to the team.

Q: A film editor said he noticed a kind of grace and strut in Michael that he can also see in Bugs Bunny.

A: There are a lot of similarities. Both have very large feet and hands. They are both quick and they jump very high. It looks like Bugs carries a bit more body fat than Michael does.

Q: What is Michael's body fat?

A: It's currently about 3 percent.

Q: Sounds like you'd better work up a plan for Bugs.

A: No problem. Would you like me to fax that to him?

The Dome was fully equipped for season training. "The machines were big enough to fit someone as small as Muggsy or as tall as Patrick," says Tim Grover, directing Jordan's workout (left). "I didn't want to make the facility strictly for Michael, but for all the professional players." Below is Bugs's regimen as dictated by Grover.

A.T.T.A.C.K. ATHLETICS
INCORPORATED

Ambition • Team Work • Achievement • Commitment • Tr

Client: Mr. Bugs Bunny	
Sex: Male	Age: N/A
Height: 42 inches	Weight: 80 lbs

Fitness Evaluation:
Excellent!

Individual evaluation test results:

No history of medical problems.
Resting Heart Rate:	60
Blood Pressure:	130/82
Body Fat Percentage:	12
Three minute Step Test:	78
PWC (Max) (kgm):	1905
VO2 (Max) (mL/kg):	63
Flexibility:	19
Bench press:	34
Sit-ups:	50

A.T.T.A.C.K. ATHLETICS
INCORPORATED

Ambition • Team Work • Achievement • Commitment • Kinetics

Client: Mr. Bugs Bunny	
Sex: Male	Age: N/A
Height: 42 inches	Weight: 80 lbs

Daily Work Out Regimen

Warm-Up:
3 to 5 minute Jog
3 to 5 minute Rope Jump

Passive Partner Stretching (Each Stretch held for 15 seconds):

Lower - Body	Upper-Body
1. Seated Straddle	6. Pectoral Stretch
2. Knees to Chest	7. Triceps Stretch
3. Lying Hamstring Stretch	8. Shoulder Stretch
4. Butterfly Stretch	9. Bicep Stretch
5. Quadriceps Stretch	10. Lat Stretch

Basketball Skills and Drills against HoopMate:
1. Right Handed Lay-Ups
2. Left Handed Lay-Ups
3. Five Spot Jump Shooting
4. Ball Handling Skills
5. Defensive Strategies

Basketball Court Conditioning Drills:
1. Suicides	5. Running Stairs
2. Reverse Suicides	6. Lateral Slide
3. Full-Court Sprints	7. Square Runs
4. Half-Court Sprints	8. Lane Run

Plyometrics:
1. Box Jump (Forward and Back)
2. Box Jump (Up and Down)
3. Box Jump (Side to Side)

Once the playing started, the action at the Dome was nonstop, and definitely not for the occasional player.

Jordan arrived at the Dome for an early morning workout, worked on the set all day, and played basketball for at least two hours a night. Here, he takes a breather during a practice game.

Spectator seats in the Dome were scarce, but those lucky enough to get in witnessed some furious preseason contests. Here, Lamont Murray (in glasses) is dogged by Cedric Ceballos, Reggie Miller, Juwan Howard, and LaSalle Thompson, while Dennis Rodman hangs back for a possible rebound.

Interview

Q & A: Hubie and Bertie

March 29, 1996. Warner Bros. Commissary.
Hubie and Bertie came out of retirement for their parts in *Space Jam*. Hubie runs a pet gourmet catering service. Bertie sells doll house furniture.

Q: How long have you two been in movies?

B: Uh, we been goin' to movies since the Truman administration. We're little, an' we get in real cheap.

H: I think she means how long we been *playin'* in movies. Listen up, will ya?

B: Yeah, yeah! Sure, sure!

H: We been a team since 1946.

Q: Um, where did you learn that announcer voice you used in the movie?

H: *Masterpiece Theatre!*

B: Master*cheese* Theatre! Yeah, yeah! Sure, sure!

H: Hey, tone it down, will ya, Bert? She's got a *tape recorder* there . . . *Ackchally*, I learned it at the YMCA. Young Mouse Cat Aggravators.

B: Riot! You got the timing, Hubie!

H: It's *all* timing!

B: Sure, sure!

4

MOVING PICTURES

Animation is much more than pictures that move.
It's an American art form in which tens of thousands
of drawings — the work of hundreds of hands —
blend to create living, breathing beings. Good
animation can startle audiences into seeing
something of themselves — even in a rabbit or a
duck. It turns characters into *performers*.

Alchemy

Animation is a misunderstood art form. It is more than the art of making pictures move; that's sequential drawing. The space between that and real animation is like the space between writing and typing. The root of animation is *anima*, soul, the breath of life. Good animation moves from the inside out.

To be an animator is to find music in common motions. To be an animator is to be comfortable in isolation, content with anonymity. To be an animator is to be a lone collaborator in an elaborate tapestry. It blends one's own work into the work of many while leaving a joyful (or wicked) individual mark somewhere in the process. Great animation is unexplainable in words, beyond skill and talent and dedication, perhaps beyond any conscious inspiration. It is the transmutation of the ordinary into the extraordinary that seems sometimes, on the face of it, even beyond the skill of the artist. Great animation is a commitment to a painstaking spontaneity at twenty-four drawings per second. Above all else, great animation is alchemy.

There is a misconception that animation is drawn by computer. Although many animation studios use computers to create and animate backgrounds (computer-generated imaging or CGI) and to make some characters move (their limited motion is a tip-off), true character animation is still created by a person with a pencil and paper. Those who are good at it are much sought-after by Hollywood.

Animation's astonishingly subtle and delicate process is like the changing of the seasons; many things have to happen, often in concert, for it to take place. Most are rudimentary and process-driven. They cannot account for the spark that fires good animation, but they are essential in setting the stage for that spark to occur. For instance, before a pencil can touch paper, each character to be animated must first have a voice, or the dialogue will look awkward and out of synch.

Calculation and instinct on a lighted pegboard.

Ideally speaking, once the storyboard and script are finished and approved, voice actors are hired to record the entire dialogue track. From the moment of his audition as a drunken bull in 1936, until his death in 1989, Mel Blanc performed the bulk of the Looney Tunes character voices, setting a standard that has been both an inspiration and

a curse. Since his death, the scramble to find voice talents who are not simply mimics but actors has seen just a few successes, and in that area, the very nature of the search deepens the appreciation for Blanc's astonishing talent. In casting the Looney Tunes characters, Ivan Reitman was adamant in his demands. "The responsibility here was to maintain their [personalities], making sure that they work today in the 1990s as well as they worked in the past," Reitman says. "One of the jobs that I felt very responsible for was to get great voices for the Looney Tunes again, voices that really sound like Mel's originals, but performed by actors who can create and go with the comedy. [Blanc] was a great actor, a great comic, so there was this wonderful sparkle in those characters. I felt some of that slipped a bit in the 1970s when they were done for television. I wanted to bring back the quality of the voices and the acting to the characters. So, we really went on a very extensive talent hunt to get these voices punchy and funny, the way they were."

That meant a wide-open audition from which it was hoped that a treasure might be found. Although most of the Looney Tunes voices had been performed for other cartoon projects since Blanc's death, no one has officially "passed the mantle" of the actor's vocal repertory company. "We started from scratch," says Joe Medjuck. "We wanted comedians who weren't afraid to act." Recording took place on a stage on the Warner lot, where the voice talents stood at five mikes and played out the scenes to each other, watching a huge video monitor that displayed the storyboard panels for inspiration. The face-to-face recording allowed the actors a sense of rhythm and tension in playing out the comedy, a luxury that the multiple-voiced Blanc seldom had.

The bulk of the *Space Jam* story is the interaction between Michael Jordan and the animated characters. From all of the footage shot on the green screen set, a black-and-white photo of every frame of film is created for the artists to animate to — a process known as photo-roto — for exact character placement. Combining these elements of photo roto images, the voice track, and the storyboard drawings, co-directors of animation Bruce Smith and Tony Cervone set down the characters' performances and the animation's pacing in the story reel, a filmed version of the storyboards with a vocal track, which assigns timings for each scene and can be watched like a movie (even though nothing is animated yet). This then acts as a map for the artists. For each scene, Cervone and Smith created sketches to denote the beginning point of action, the ending point, and the stops along the way, accompanied by suggested poses. They also designate how many frames to allow for vowel sounds and mouth movements in speaking scenes (which is why the dialogue track must be recorded first). Despite their dictates, the story reel and directors' sketches still allow an animator enormous leeway in creating movement and expression in a scene.

Actor Kath Soucie gives a voice to Lola Bunny.

Cervone, an affable Chicagoan with a boisterous, straight-razor wit, and Smith, a soft-spoken, insightful L.A. native, share a common philosophy of giving the artists direction, then encouraging them to add their personal stamp to the way the scene is played within the space given. Joe Pytka praises the directors' eye for the characters. "[Cervone and Smith] made them more . . . *breathing*," Pytka explains. "The way they drew everything was a little hipper, a little edgier, and a little rougher [than the original storyboard art]."

Reitman was looking for the kind of irrepressible style associated with Warner Bros. cartoons. "They're [characters] with faults and anger and irony and silliness, all working together in sort of a real fireball way." This "fireball" manner, which was mostly a matter of tone in the six-minute cartoons, became an actual animation style for *Space Jam*. Pytka's wild camera put new demands on the animators to view Bugs and the other characters in ways they had never before been seen. While this was helped by 3-D models of the characters, the vision and execution of their movement came completely from the animators and their directors.

The characters had previously been photographed by a stationary animation camera in front of a flat proscenium, moving left to right, foreground to background, but have never before been followed by a camera, which moves around them as they move to follow the unpredictable live-action movements of an athlete like Michael Jordan. "What does the top of Bugs Bunny's head look like?" Tony Cervone asks rhetorically to illustrate the choices the artists were faced with. "What does he look like when he's turning to get out of the way of a moving camera, or from below as the camera follows him when he jumps?"

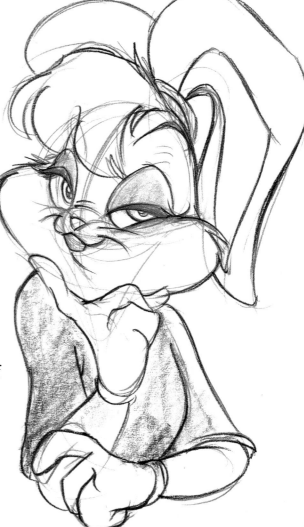

As the scenes are timed and assigned, the art director, Bill Perkins, working with the producers and directors, begins planning the animation's "look," especially the backgrounds and environments. For *Space Jam*, this early step was critical, because Michael Jordan would be moving around and interacting within an animated environment. These are not simple character-against-a-background shots, but advanced technology — "2 3/4-D" as the visual effects people call it — designed to convince the audience that Jordan is actually *in* an animated world, not stuck on top of one.

Not since *Who Framed Roger Rabbit* had there been a film requiring such daunting specialized artistic skill. Warner Bros. went to a man well known for his expertise at marshalling a crew large enough to handle *Space Jam*, longtime Disney veteran Max Howard, who was a member of the *Roger Rabbit* team. Once again, Howard found himself back in the intertwining worlds of animation and live action. "*Roger Rabbit* pushed the boundaries then," Howard says, "but now, all these years later, through the developments in digital filmmaking, what was considered the 'cutting edge' in *Roger Rabbit* would now be thought of as pedestrian." Howard speaks of animators and artists with an affection bordering on awe, and recalls the moment when he first met the animation crew.

"I thought, *Oh! you're actors! Of course you are!* What I understood was that a good animator is like a good actor. It comes down to a word called timing — the look in the eye, the gesture. To master the subtle movement and that little look at just the right moment is what separates the good and the brilliant." The subtle gesture that reflects personality, the pause between frantic actions, the shift in the eye that broadcasts a character's inner psychology — these were the things that make the Looney Tunes-style animation distinctly different from Disney. This innate mastery is something of a sixth sense for animators, something they aren't eager to talk about, but which is very clear to a director observing their work.

The producers pulled together about 100 Warner Bros. Animation artists (working on TV and Classic Animation department projects) and "borrowed" another 200 from Warner Bros. Feature Animation (the assembled group became *Space Jam* Animation, and included assistant animators, layout artists, and background artists), plus another 60 artists hired just for the movie, and more than 400 artists in satellite studios around the United States (Character Builders, Inc. in Columbus, Ohio, Heart of Texas Productions, Inc. in Austin, Texas, Rainbow Animation Group in

Glendale, California, Spaff Animation in North Hollywood, California), Canada (Charles Gammage Animation, Inc., London), England (Uli Meyer Features, Ltd., Premier Films, Stardust Pictures, and Warner Bros. Feature Animation, London), and Dublin, Ireland (Monster Productions). With only eleven months until the film's release date and no rough animation complete, Max Howard quickly summoned Ron Tippe, a longtime friend and Disney colleague, to step in, grab the oars of the film's production, and navigate the animation group through the exhausting but ultimately exhilarating months ahead. Cervone and Smith, who played integral roles during the live-action shoot assisting Joe Pytka with character placement and posing, were assigned to direct the work of all satellite studios and coordinate the core unit in Sherman Oaks.

Using fax machine, teleconferences, phone calls, video tapes, and personal visits, Tippe was able to inspire in his staff (between the diverse studios and different levels of participation) an *esprit d'corps* sustained all the way through the final days of production. "Most of producing is setting attitude," he says, relaxing in his office after another grueling week. "It's setting goals that are attainable and providing an atmosphere for the crew that is as fun and tension-free as possible, given that these jobs come with [built-in] tensions. I don't micromanage," he admits. "My goal is to remain as objective as possible — keep an overview."

While handling the myriad administrative duties of a producer, Tippe has made a point of avoiding the sanctuary of his office, preferring instead to spend much of each day walking amongst the animators' and layout artists' workplaces and soliciting suggestions and gripes. "A pat on the back, a stop at a desk to say 'you're doing a great job' goes a long way," says Tippe, who, like Max Howard, enjoys inspiring (but never distracting) his artists. "It's very heartening to see someone sitting alone with the character and a blank sheet of paper: drawing, erasing, drawing, flipping pages, looking in a mirror, asking questions of the characters as they might ask of themselves. It's not just a matter of proficiency — it's great commitment and passion."

Jerry Rees agrees. "When animators are looking truly into a performance, the top players really understand it's about capturing what a moment feels like instead of what

it looks like," he declares. "You know when people say [of a caricature], 'It looks more like him than the real person,' what a crazy statement that is, but that's what you're trying to do with performance and animation. You're trying to make [the character's qualities] feel more strong. The actor comes out in the animator."

Alone with their scene assignments and their pencils, the artists translate their experiences and their individual takes on life, envisioning — then creating — Bugs Bunny's actions, Daffy Duck's reactions, Lola Bunny's athletic grace, the Monstars' athletic brutality. To achieve the nearly 40,000 finished pictures in the movie, feature animation went through more than a million sheets of paper (which was recycled). When the film is complete, the work of one Bugs Bunny artist blends seamlessly into the work of another, and it all becomes Bugs, the artists' personalities dissolving into the character's own and becoming a part of it. In the end, the audience believes in Bugs, unaware that perhaps four dozen men and women have breathed the life into him for this film. "We're not only looking for uniformity and consistency in execution, but also in breadth of portrayal," says Ron Tippe.

Bruce Smith, co-director of animation, asserts that "the real challenge of the animator is to grab what the essence of the character is, based on what is established from the past. That's a hard thing, because you're providing light into the character. It doesn't matter how well it's drawn, no matter how good it looks, if that character doesn't act like Bugs or look like Bugs, people know. If it doesn't have the soul of Bugs, you've lost it."

A frame at a time, from studio to studio, the rough animation reaches completion. The scenes are "cleaned up" in the assistant animation stage and handed over to the animation effects department, where the tones, highlights, and shadows are added to prepare the characters for compositing. The drawings are then checked by hand and scanned into the computer system, where they are inked and painted digitally. After months of encountering and clearing obstacles, the makers of *Space Jam*'s next monumental challenge will be met five miles from Warner Bros. at a visual effects studio called Cinesite, where the ephemeral is transformed into the digital.

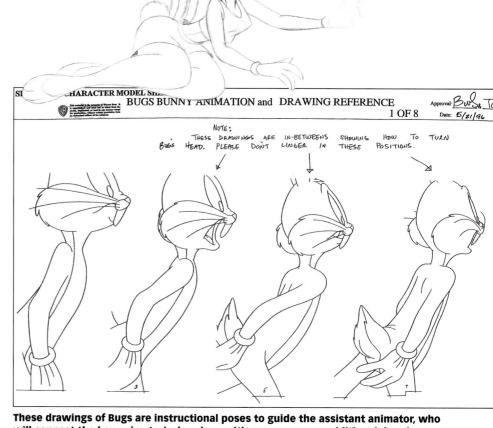

Character references

When dozens of animators are working on scenes involving the same character (Bugs, for instance), they require a guide to help them give him the consistent look of a single artist. These guides, called model sheets, dictate the style in which Bugs (and his cohorts) must be drawn. Model sheets are drawn by the animation director (or a trusted artist), and usually include a variety of facial expressions, a proportion sketch, action poses, and a turnaround. Even though the animators are working with exactly the same style Bugs, their individual personalities come through in the way he moves and the expressions he displays. A director can easily tell which animator has drawn a scene simply by looking at it, the artist's individual personality coming through in the choices he or she makes for playing Bugs's actions in the scene.

These drawings of Bugs are instructional poses to guide the assistant animator, who will connect the key animator's drawings with any necessary additional drawings.

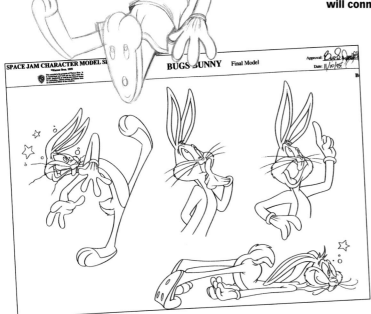

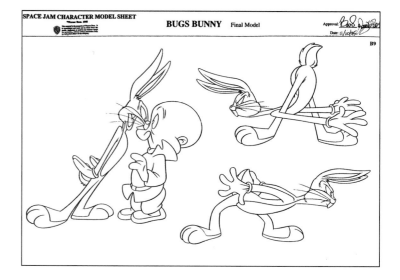

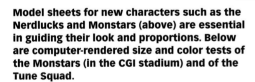

Tony Cervone (left) and Bruce Smith are the film's co-directors of animation, overseers of an international effort. Here, they confer over a flexible maquette of Bugs, used for positioning during the scene in the Jordan home.

Model sheets for new characters such as the Nerdlucks and Monstars (above) are essential in guiding their look and proportions. Below are computer-rendered size and color tests of the Monstars (in the CGI stadium) and of the Tune Squad.

Motion control

Artists were ordered to pull out all the stops when animating the characters for *Space Jam*, exaggerating their movements and going for the laughs. This resulted in the clownish Sylvester (a throwback to Friz Freleng's original vision for him) and Tweety's martial arts posture, a thoroughly modern but completely in-character stance for the little canary with the big sense of self-preservation.

A storyboard adjustment reflects a new idea for a gag. Left to right: Gary Mouri, Bill Perkins, Fred Cline, Bruce Smith, Tony Cervone, and Ron Tippe.

The key animator draws poses at various stages of an action (below), and the assistant (often called an "in-betweener") follows the action through between poses, using the director's timing sheet to determine in what space of time the action must take place.

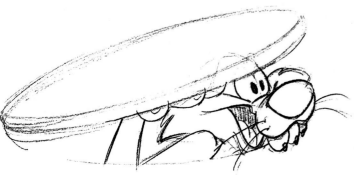

Ron Tippe, the film's animation producer, held regular meetings during the film's production, keeping track of an army of artists and technicians and tracking the progress of the animation and composition, and its merger with the live-action footage.

Bruce Smith, Todd Winter, and Gary Mouri review a layout sketch.

A film like *Space Jam* (and a game like basketball) put new demands on the skills of artists drawing familiar characters in unfamiliar poses and situations. The spirit and raw energy of an animator's sketches (which will be in-betweened to fill in the movement) are clear in these two poses of Taz going to the hoop.

Rough and ready

Nothing so completely documents the spirit of a scene like the artist's first sketches. The style of the lines, their urgency, the pressure of the pencil on the paper, the animator's own sense of the character — all of these are clear in the rough drawings. The picture itself is almost a by-product of the scene the artist has playing in his or her mind. What animators fear most for their work is the stiffening of it through the cleanup, inking, and painting processes. But a good cleanup artist knows how to retain the variations of line width in the original sketch and tries to preserve that quality. In the old days, each picture was meticulously hand inked on a celluloid sheet, then hand painted. Today, the process is done electronically — scanned into a computer and "painted" with a special software program. While it benefits the production in its speed, the modern process eliminates production cels, which are popular among collectors.

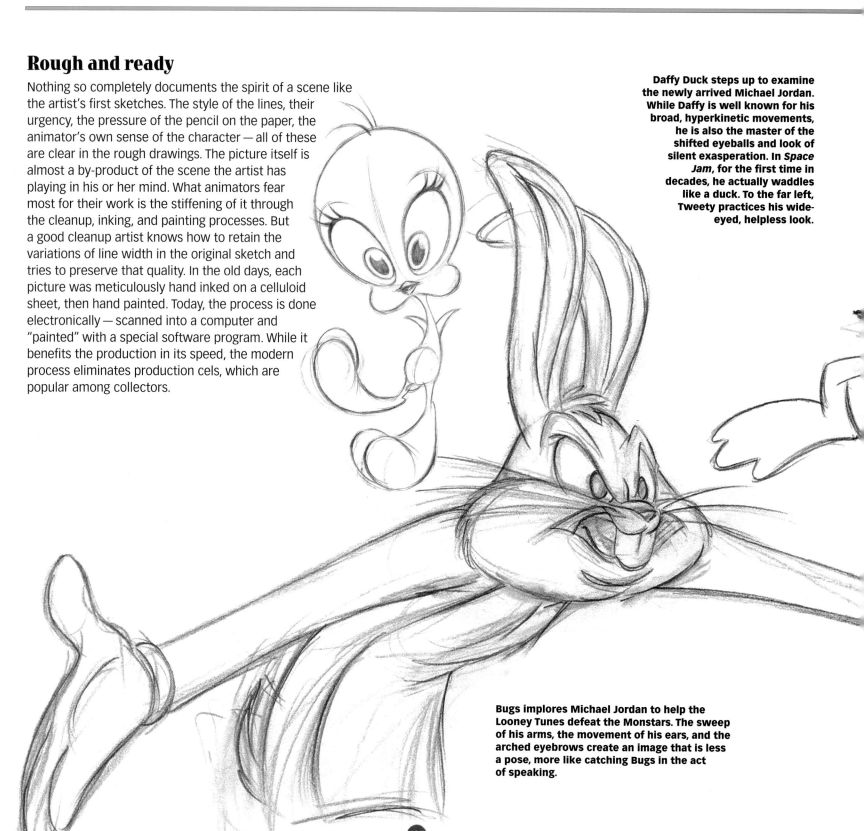

Daffy Duck steps up to examine the newly arrived Michael Jordan. While Daffy is well known for his broad, hyperkinetic movements, he is also the master of the shifted eyeballs and look of silent exasperation. In *Space Jam*, for the first time in decades, he actually waddles like a duck. To the far left, Tweety practices his wide-eyed, helpless look.

Bugs implores Michael Jordan to help the Looney Tunes defeat the Monstars. The sweep of his arms, the movement of his ears, and the arched eyebrows create an image that is less a pose, more like catching Bugs in the act of speaking.

Interview

Q & A: Foghorn Leghorn

May 24, 1996, Las Vegas, Nevada. Foghorn is a bit smaller than he appears on film, but he makes up for it with arm gestures. He's at the Warner Bros. Studio Store, making an appearance, but is taking a quiet moment in the stock room.

Q: Is there anyplace you can go that doesn't cause a ruckus?

A: Washing, ah-say, Washington. D.C., that is. Hardly stand out at all.

Q: To what do you attribute your longevity?

A: A return, as a nation, to vegetarianism.

Q: Really?

A: That's a joke, son! Y'too serious, boy — hidebound! Gotta relax, ah-say relax! (Kid's so tight his shoulder blades is rubbin' together.) Take a deep breath! You're tighter than a snake-charmer's basket! Loosen up! Have a ball! Basket, ball. Basketball! That's another joke, son! *Space Jam*, that is.

Q: Is there anyplace a guy like you can't go?

A: Well, I got tossed, ah-say tossed, out of the Siegfried and Roy Show. Didn't do a thing! Said I was distractin' the cats, but I'm much tamer than I used t'be and that's no lyin'. Lyin', tamer. Lion-tamer! Breathe, boy! I'm holdin' up the hoop but you're not jumpin' through!

123

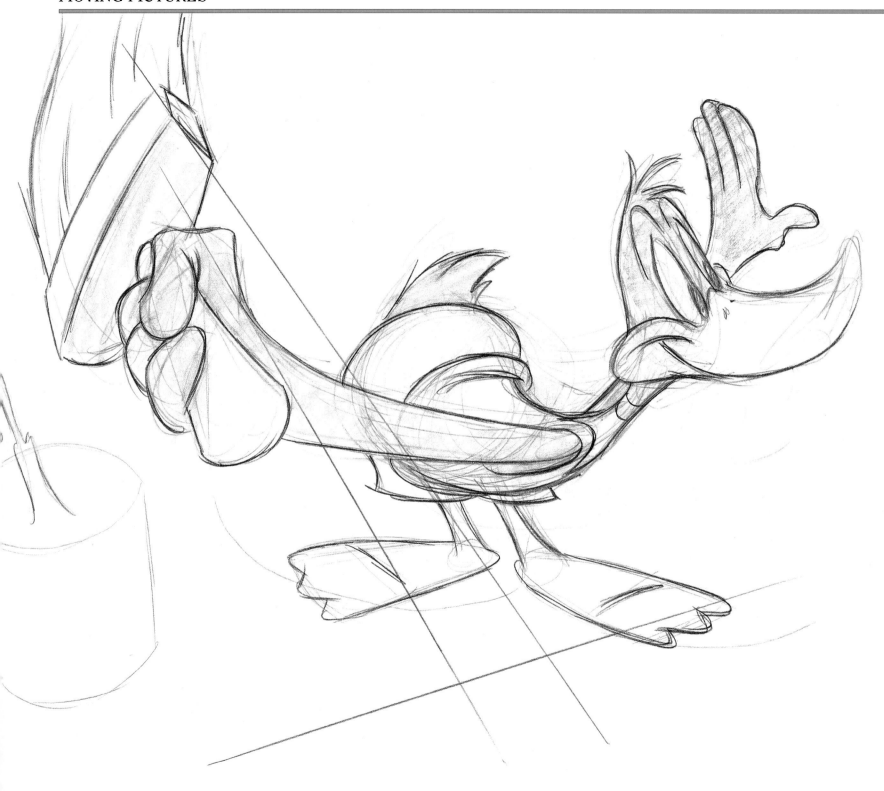

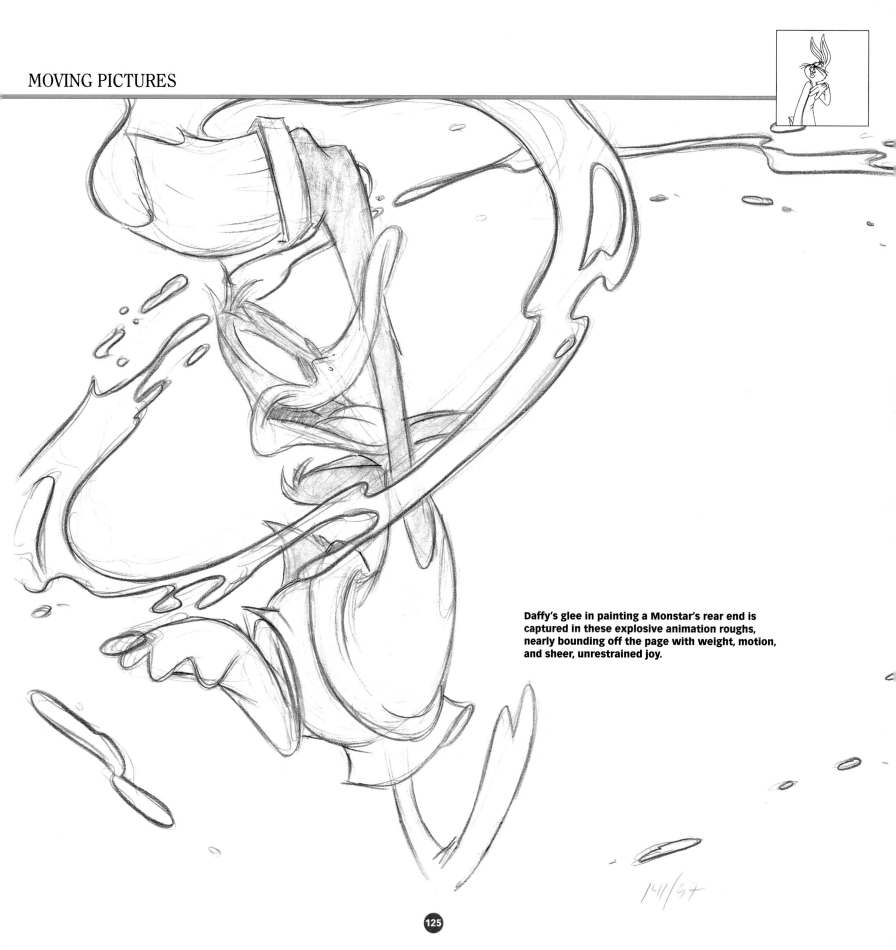

Daffy's glee in painting a Monstar's rear end is captured in these explosive animation roughs, nearly bounding off the page with weight, motion, and sheer, unrestrained joy.

Interview

Q & A with Ron Tippe

July 5, 1996. Space Jam Animation, Sherman Oaks, California.
Ron Tippe is animation producer for *Space Jam*. His pace is harried,
but within his tidy office, he is able to make a visitor feel completely
relaxed. His tortoise shell glasses and intent manner give him a
professorial air.

Q: What was your biggest concern stepping into the producer's shoes
when you did?

A: We had a compressed schedule to begin with — ten months as
opposed to two years — and had to sort out what was done and
what had to be done, in the allotted time, with the allotted budget.
Plus, 906 people have worked on the movie, so . . .

*His sentence is interrupted by a shriek from the next office. Tippe
doesn't miss a beat.*

A: 905! The question was, How do you get 906 people, spread
over six thousand miles, all talking the same visual language?
That was the greatest challenge.

Q: And it was met.

A: (He lets out a long breath.) The rough animation for the whole
film was finished in just short of six months, and I think that's
rather amazing, especially for a movie this visually complex.

Q: What's your guiding philosophy as a producer?

A: Never come to me with a problem without having a solution. I
believe in a proactive point of view in giving people a say in
solving their own problems. With all these [satellite] studios, we
sometimes felt we were forced to react. So we took the initiative to
resolve potential problems rather than wait for them to arise.

Q: What words come to mind to
describe your animators?

A: I see extremely hard-
working, passionate,
committed artists who are more
concerned with bringing the life
of the character forward than
anything else. It requires great
thought about what every frame
is going to look like without an
overview of the entire movie.
They become the character,
and in doing so achieve an
emotional connection with
the audience.

Putting words in their mouths

Mel Blanc, who performed most of the voices during Looney Tunes' Golden Age, recorded each character's voice track separately; they were edited together later. "What people don't understand about Mel Blanc is that he was an amazing actor," explains Bob Bergen, the voice of Porky Pig and Tweety, who as a microphone-struck fourteen-year-old called Blanc at home for career advice. "His acting sticks out more for me than his voice, because each character has a distinct personality." The voice actors for *Space Jam,* inspired by (but not imitating) Blanc's work, were able to play scenes against each other, giving the work a sense of dynamism and playful tension. In casting the voices, Reitman sought actors who could bring an actor's rather than a mimic's vocal qualities to the roles. It is a testament to Blanc's artistry that, after his death, a wide-ranging search was necessary to find voices for the roles that originated with him.

As a monitor displays the storyboard panels, voice actors Bill Farmer, Kath Soucie, and Dee Bradley Baker listen to direction for a scene.

Danny DeVito is as animated as his character, the villain Swackhammer.

Tough work if you can get it

Animating a character into a live-action sequence is nothing unusual, but the directors want every close interaction between animated and living actor to look authentic. This is achieved through the photo-roto process. The misty nature of the photo makes it simpler for the animator, since it makes the details less distracting.

Frederika Keston, the set actor for Lola Bunny, steps in for Bugs's kissing scene with Michael Jordan, establishing an eyeline with the actor. The photo-roto is used merely as a placement guide for the artist animating Bugs.

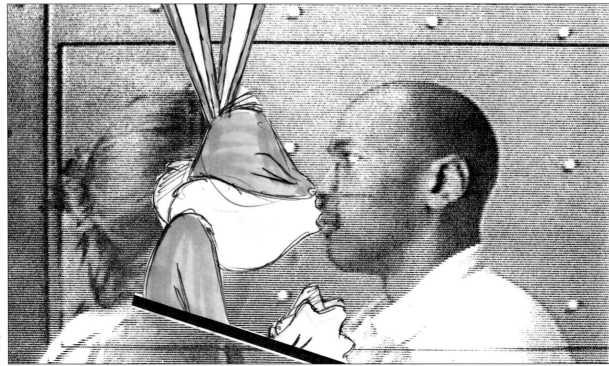

On the set, the animators draw Bugs on top of Keston's image, providing a visual guide for the director.

The rough animation sketch of the kiss captures Bugs in all his lovably sarcastic splendor.

The cleaned up animation drawing of the top sketch will be "inked" and "painted" in the computer and sent by phone line to Cinesite for compositing. Below, the original storyboard panel illustrates the animator's early conception of the shot.

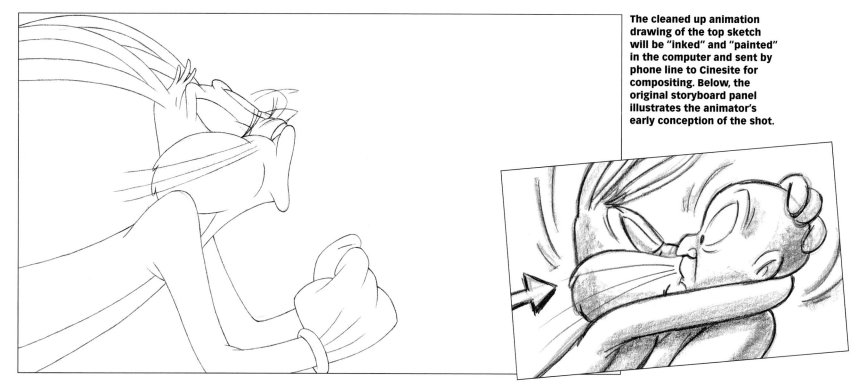

5

WHEN WORLDS COLLIDE

Animation + computer-generated imaging = virtual fun for the audience, but it took long hours and heroic measures of patience to pull off Michael Jordan's trip to Looney Tune Land.

Virtuality

When Bugs Bunny passes the ball to Michael Jordan, or Jordan is checked by one of the brutish Monstars, or he holds Tweety in the palm of his hand, Ed Jones crosses his fingers. He's hoping no one is cheering his work, at least not till after the final credits roll. The visual effects wizard and president of the visual effects house Cinesite is well aware of the irony that, in a business fueled by the clamor for recognition, he is for this moment hoping for some anonymity. "Audiences have to believe that animation and live action coexist and coexist seamlessly, to the point that they don't have to think or want to think why this is happening," Jones says.

Jones won an Academy Award in 1989 for his work on *Who Framed Roger Rabbit*, and while there is a temptation to compare *Space Jam* and *Roger Rabbit*, the two are fundamentally different in style, approach, and especially technology. *Roger Rabbit* is essentially a story of *animated* characters functioning in the real world. The movie was shot against elaborate sets, with the physical interaction between the animation and the live action accounted for in the optical manipulation of the live-action elements.

In *Space Jam*, though, virtually all of the interaction between live actors and the Looney Tunes characters occurs in a completely animated environment, with Michael Jordan on *animated* turf, not vice versa. Sixteen minutes and thirty-three seconds of this animation play out during the heat of a basketball game, with Jordan the featured player amongst an animated group of costars. While the Cinesite team has created effects for dozens of

Joe Pytka's roving wild camera puts demands on not only the animators, but the special effects team, which has to create a virtual "2¾-D" environment within which the actors — living and animated — can perform. These storyboard panels reflect Joe Pytka's vision for the kinds of shots he wants in the animation.

high-profile feature films, Jones calls *Space Jam* "the largest effects film ever," not because of its magnitude or explosiveness, but because the effect has to be sustained with absolute consistency through hundreds of shots over sixty-five minutes of visual effects film. It's a tall order and a thankless one. "There are no extra points for degree of difficulty," quips Joe Medjuck.

A film like *Space Jam* could not have been made five years ago because the technology that could capture Michael Jordan's fiery playing instincts or director Joe Pytka's visceral, spur-of-the-moment camera style had not yet been created. Before, in order to play Jordan off of animated characters, the film would have required a live-action setting. Jordan's movements would have been

choreographed with absolute precision and filmed with a "locked down" motion control camera so if more than a single take was required (as it always is), he could repeat exactly what he had done before. Only then could it be successfully merged with the animation. But Pytka doesn't work that way, and neither does Jordan. "There's only one take," Jordan told Ed Jones, "and I only do it once because I can never repeat what I just did. I never know what I'm going to do."

Back in the earliest development stages, Jones and his crew strategized how they could realistically place Michael Jordan in the midst of Looney Tune Land without his looking like an isolated element dropped into an animated movie. Ironically, against finely rendered fully animated characters, there was more of a risk of *Jordan* looking two-dimensional, not the characters. Jones was preparing to test his newest technology, a filming technique and computer program so unusual that virtually no one else in the business had ever used them at this volume. It was (and is) a groundbreaking motion-tracking process by which a background environment could be created and put in place that would move as the camera moves, following the action of the players. All of it would be pulled off in a computer. It sounded like a backward way to shoot a movie; Jones believed it was the *only* way to shoot this one. The explosive, instinctive styles of Jordan and Joe

Ed Jones of Cinesite speaks to the digital filmmaking process: "We're trying to create a process which will be applied to filmmaking in the future. We shoot the actors in front of the screen so you can put them in any environment you want to later on; we keep the camera moving (and we keep the continuity). We're staking out territory here in a way that's groundbreaking, but will eventually become the way movies are made."

Pytka seemed to work counter to the precisely calculated, no-reshoot world of animation. "This was a basketball game after all, and it's a very fast-moving sport. So it behooved us to have the opportunity to move the camera in that way," Jones admits. He was responsible for bringing together the visions of the producer, the director, the star, and the feature animation team. He knew his crew could pull it off, but since the technology that would tie everything together was new and untested on a project of this magnitude, its success was still speculative.

On Soundstage 22 at the Warner Bros. lot, designers created a huge set without a horizon plane and painted it an eye-wearying bright green. "It's not meant to be pretty," admits Jones, noting that Jordan's skin coloring and the color of the Tune Squad uniform against green (as opposed to blue or white) "allowed us to extract better mattes to separate Michael [from the background]."

Still smiling after all these frames: Some of the Cinesite visual effects crew. From left: Doug Tubach, Mitzi Gallagher, Ed Jones, and Carlos Arguello.

Red balls, each carrying a legible reference number, were hot-glued to the backdrop in a four-by-four-foot grid. "These were reference points for us to build a virtual environment of a gym, in the computer." Jones could then track from the computer how the camera moved after the fact, and how it related to the balls. From this, a background could be created in the computer that would realistically move to match the movements of the characters in front of it. All of Jordan's scenes with the

animated characters were shot against this simple green screen set. The actors, swathed in green suits and masks, acted out the parts of the animated characters which allowed Jordan to make and sustain eye contact, an extraordinarily difficult task for the actor but an essential part of the illusion's success.

After all of the scenes were shot, everything green would be removed, leaving only Michael Jordan playing to the empty air around him. This isolated image of Jordan began as a single element, but by the film's end, it would be a part of dozens of overlays and processes applied to the animation. As a lone element, it could be repositioned easily in the computer to harmonize with the other elements on the screen. Visual harmony became the goal.

As the filming progressed, animators from Cinesite (whom Jones calls "visualists," since they actually built the environment in which the action would take place) and Warner Bros. Feature Animation worked closely with Joe Pytka on the set. Pytka would set up a shot, photograph it, and hand it over to the animators, who would sketch their vision of how the environment would play into the scene. "We haven't chosen the location yet," Jones said at the time, "but we've already shot the action, and we're going to put it into the location once we build it." The location would, of course, have certain elements common to gymnasiums and stadiums, and

This is a computer-generated model of the stadium for the Ultimate Game. During the course of its design, the size and capacity changed (from 8,000 seats to 25,000), requiring a whole new strategy for its conception. It is primarily modeled after the Great Western Forum in Los Angeles, although Jones and his crew studied many arenas in American cities and incorporated much of what they found into their design.

these were accounted for during the live-action shoot. If the artists envisioned a window in the practice gym, for instance, the director would order Jordan lighted and then film to account for that. At this stage, the start-and-stop and patience-testing waiting time while the director and crew considered angles and backgrounds began to take its toll. But in the end, everyone was assured, the wait will have been worth it.

Once each frame of the film was reproduced as a misty black-and-white photograph (sharp lines are harder for animators to work with), animators could begin their magic. Once approved, the completed animation — inked and painted on computers — was scanned into a digital electronic file and then transferred to videotape for editing. The film was immediately transferred to this digital format

then loaded onto videotape, from which the effects would be composed; when the process is finished, all of the video is transferred back to film.

In another Cinesite department, the visualists had been creating for months a virtual environment for the animated portion of the film, using "wire-frame" models. Most challenging were the two key settings needed for the principal animated scenes: a Looney Tunes practice gym, and a large basketball stadium to act as the site of the Ultimate Game. Inspired by a high school gym in New York, the Cinesite crew "built" its own gym in the computer, using the wire-frame skeleton to create a three-dimensional model. This acted as a blueprint for the building. Once the frame was created the computer could virtually mold "texture maps" (wood, concrete, plaster, etc.) over the flat surfaces in much the same way a child would use chicken wire and papier-maché to create a three-dimensional object. "It's like creating a virtual set in the computer," explains Cinesite's digital producer Scott Dougherty. Utilizing an astonishing piece of technology, the computer could "fly" its own inner 3-D "camera" to specific areas within the structure and frame them on the screen from any position. The correct perspective was adjusted automatically, since the dimensions of every square inch of the structure are built into the computer's memory. The digital artists then detailed the scene, rendering a photo-realistic virtual environment.

In the Cinesite offices, the expensive high-tech elements are surrounded by the pleasant low-tech clutter of mugs, paper clip dispensers, a Daffy Duck figurine, a glass bowl of pistachios, which softens the technology and acts as a reminder of who actually operates the machines. The animation is being prepared for compositing, a step that brings all the layers together and visually matches them so they look like they were photographed through a single camera. In some scenes, layer upon layer of elements must be pulled together. The digital composite supervisor, Doug Tubach, takes flat two-dimensional forms of each animated character, Michael Jordan, Wayne Knight, props, special effects, and lighting changes, and sculpts them into three-dimensional elements (the animation department provides to Cinesite half-tones and shadows that are layered in during final compositing). If a single element is under- or overdone, it ruins the effect. If Michael Jordan's positioning and lighting aren't exactly consistent with the other characters and their surrounding environment, the human eye will find the mistake — perhaps not consciously — creating a troubling discrepancy that can keep the audience from totally suspending its disbelief.

It's a complicated process, combining the real world with the animated one.

In a darkened room, illuminated by the soft light of a monitor screen, Scott Dougherty points to an image of Michael Jordan sitting on the grass in Looney Tune Land, bewildered and surrounded by animated characters. Porky Pig is in the foreground, blurred, his back to the audience. "We take an animated character like Porky Pig and apply real-life camera techniques. Since he's in the foreground, he's out of focus. The shadow of Tweety is something that we added [fluttering] over Michael and the [other] animated characters so they appear to be standing in the same space, creating a sense that they're together."

These elements are laid over each other electronically, like clear sheets of celluloid. A single shot like this, which is just a few seconds of film, can take two days to composite.

"Everything is a separate element," Ed Jones explains. "The shadows and the light that could be cast off are separate elements. So any specific animated character could have four to six different elements [involved in] the sculpting of that character. When you look at a scene with seven different characters, times

four that's twenty-eight different elements, plus the backgrounds, which may have different levels, and we break those down to give them weight dimensionally. So there's another four, so that's thirty-two, plus Michael — that's thirty-three elements before we even put them together and start playing with them to integrate them."

Add to this the speed and intensity of basketball. "There couldn't be a more complex game to animate," Jones declares, referring to the action on the court, along with the separate show going on outside the court. "When you watch an NBA game, there's lots of different lights going off, flashbulbs going off, motion blur going on in the background — all that is happening and [it] shows depth." The Cinesite team has to account for all of this, in addition to the action of the actors and characters. "There's so much moving around," adds Jones, "that if they can't play ball *together*, it doesn't look like a real ball game."

The stadium for the Ultimate Game turned out to be the *ultimate decision*, going from an 8,000–seat venue to 25,000 seats in one quick statement from Ivan Reitman. "So now the set has 25,000 people [in the background], and there's a lot of decision-making significance to that." The bulk of the non–Looney Tunes characters in the seats must

also be animated in the computer. Researching and borrowing elements from stadiums in Orlando and

Here, Bugs's image is integrated into the virtual reality environment of the stadium. His shadows and tones were added last to "sculpt" his two-dimensional form to match the multidimensional CGI background.

Chicago, Jones's Ultimate Stadium is modeled mostly after Los Angeles's own Great Western Forum.

The final success of all this work is up to the judgement of the the audience, but from the initial completed scenes coming out of Cinesite, the illusion is working on a grand scale. The painstaking planning and time-eating effort have produced a movie whose multiple layers of complex parts are undetectable.

For instance, the locker room backgrounds were truly impressive, and could not be distinguished from a full-sized, union-built set, had the truth not been known. "We were asked to make them seem less realistic," Jones chuckles. "That's true. We had to tone them down." Despite the hassle, he called it "the best compliment any animator could be given."

Leon Schlesinger (who sold the animation studio to Jack Warner in 1943) bids Porky good luck, then listens half-heartedly as Daffy Duck pleads with him to make him a star.

In the Warner Bros. tradition

Space Jam, of course, isn't the first film to merge live action with animation. Back in 1940, Warner Bros. animation director Friz Freleng brought Porky Pig and Daffy Duck literally off the animation tables and into the real Warner Bros. studio world with *You Ought to Be in Pictures*. The live actors mimed their actions with the to-be-animated characters, and the picture was a great success. Shooting it in black and white (most likely an economic decision) added to the realistic look of the film, in which Daffy Duck convinces Porky to find a career in live-action movies, moving him aside for Daffy to take over as Warner Bros.' brightest animated star (Bugs Bunny's debut was still two months away). The naive Porky buys into Daffy's plan, getting himself chased all over the studio lot.

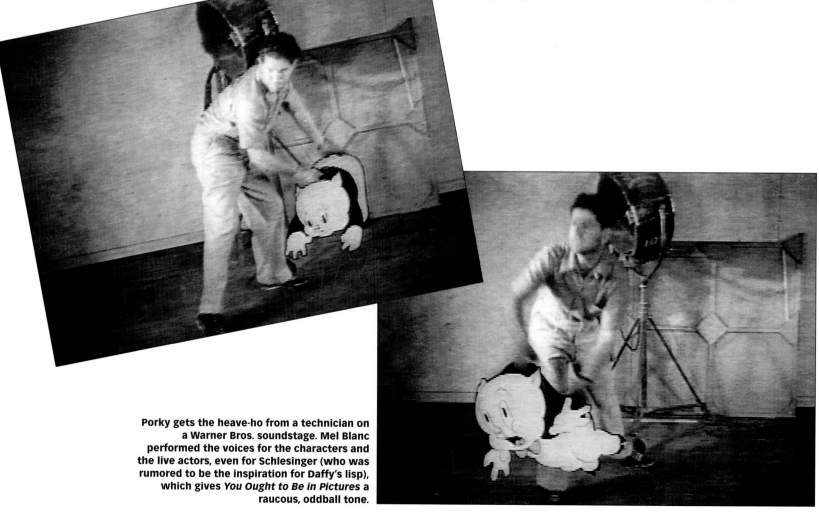

Porky gets the heave-ho from a technician on a Warner Bros. soundstage. Mel Blanc performed the voices for the characters and the live actors, even for Schlesinger (who was rumored to be the inspiration for Daffy's lisp), which gives *You Ought to Be in Pictures* a raucous, oddball tone.

The sum of the parts

What makes a film like *Space Jam* successful is the undetectable synergy of its separate parts. The audience has to be so convinced of the authenticity of what's happening that they aren't thinking about it. The three primary elements — live action, animation, and backgrounds/environments — are created separately, but the end result must be perfectly balanced that no single effect overrides the others.

THE LIVE-ACTION IMAGE
The actors must be clearly interacting with the animation, establishing eye lines and being consistently involved with action that isn't taking place at the time of filming.

THE ANIMATED CHARACTER ART
The animators are responsible for the characters' reactions to the actors, gauging and timing their mannerisms to match the actions of their costars, and appear every bit as alive. Animation artists also "lay in" shading and light source elements, which are used in Cinesite's compositing.

THE BACKGROUNDS/ENVIRONMENTS
Some of the backgrounds, such as this one, are painted; others, such as the stadium and gymnasium, are complete virtual environments. In either case, the backgrounds must accommodate the players and carry out the illusion that they are in them, not on them.

Virtually undetectable

Michael Jordan's moves during the film's game sequences are spontaneous and authentic. To pull this off, the backgrounds against which he plays had to be created at Cinesite after the filming. The special process used to create virtual environments for the animated segments of the film became a complicated challenge to the movie's layout artists. "[Normally] they give you the layout first and you animate to that," says Gary Mouri, layout supervisor. "Here, they do the animation [first] and then the layout person has to figure the background out behind the characters — where the ground plane is, what's behind it, what's the geography [etc.]." Cinesite then generates a nearly three-dimensional environment, giving the scene an astonishingly realistic look which allows Jordan and the Looney Tunes to occupy, believably, the same dimension.

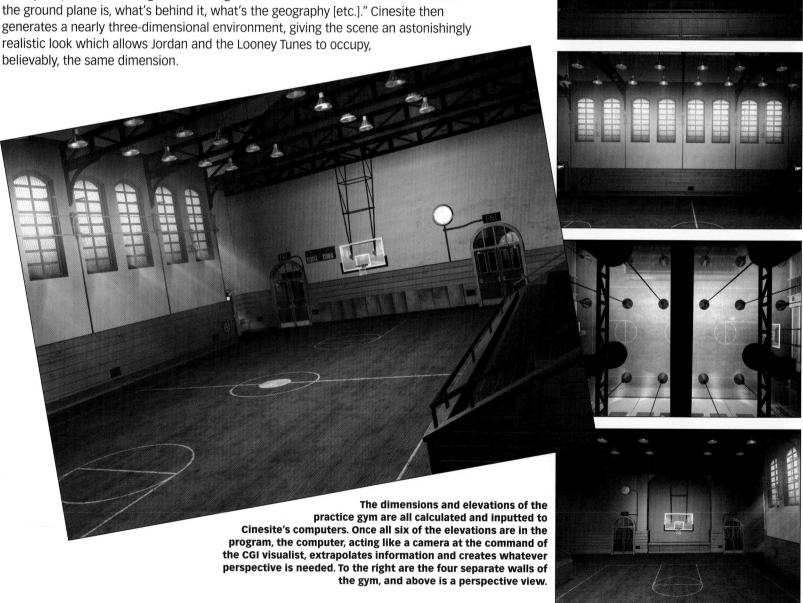

The dimensions and elevations of the practice gym are all calculated and inputted to Cinesite's computers. Once all six of the elevations are in the program, the computer, acting like a camera at the command of the CGI visualist, extrapolates information and creates whatever perspective is needed. To the right are the four separate walls of the gym, and above is a perspective view.

Michael is "sized" against both his opponents and his teammates in a size relationship test of the CGI background. The compositing process will insert many more elements including authentic light sources and shadows on the film.

The computer "camera" can even look straight up from center court, which is the origin of this underside shot of the scoreboard at the stadium.

Getting it together

Tightly edited film footage of the green screen photography is threaded into the digital film scanner, which translates it into a digital image on videotape. This image is then duplicated numerous times in each visual effects department while the original film is preserved and protected. The finished footage is later transferred back to film.

A section of film is loaded into the digital film scanner (top). Scanning operator Bob Fernley keeps track of the footage being scanned, which is measured by frame since it is a prohibitively expensive process. No more than one extra frame at the beginning and end of each session is allowed. Animation directors select movements and call the angles before scanning, matching the action to the moving backgrounds. The selected material is then loaded into the scanner.

The original green screen image, now a high-resolution digital scan, is imported to Cinesite's computer system as the first step in the compositing process.

(below) Composite supervisor Doug Tubach electronically erases the red balls from the green screen background. The next step is to add the computer-generated environment, followed by the intricate compositing process. (right) Carlos Arguello, who creates 3-D environments and lighting, reviews some stills of his work to make a color scheme choice.

The isolated image is inserted into the 3-D CGI environment, which acts as a computer "set" for the action.

Jordan is placed in the environment (shown on its own above), with Cinesite's visual effects artists digitally adjusting the light sources, shading, and color.

WHEN WORLDS COLLIDE!

Ed Jones suggests a change to Doug Tubach, who is compositing an image of Michael Jordan and the Looney Tunes within a CGI environment. During this process, the digital artist visually sculpts the screen image to bring it from two to almost three dimensions.

Dough Tubach puts the finishing touches on the frame shown below.

After Jordan's image is placed in the correct position, the characters — already animated, inked, and painted — are placed. This finished frame of Michael Jordan turning to face down the Monstars incorporates all three key elements of the compositing process — the computer-generated background, live action, and animated art.

Interview

Q & A: Ed Jones

September 12, 1995 and March 18, 1996, Cinesite, Los Angeles. Ed Jones's work has been seen in fourteen of the top twenty highest-grossing movies of all time. His company has also created visual effects for *Mission Impossible, Backdraft, Raiders of the Lost Ark, Ghostbusters,* and *Ghostbusters II.*

Q: As far as technology goes, what makes *Space Jam* different from *Roger Rabbit*?

A: This will be the first time that digital technology has been used, as opposed to traditional optical technology that was used in *Roger.* It's given us complete freedom as to how we photograph this movie. It's as if we're shooting a real basketball game with guys having cameras on their shoulders. It allows us to bring a documentary approach to the photographic images, even though we're going to combine all the [live-action, animation, and computer] elements later on.

Q: Did Michael Jordan have to move differently to leave room for the animation that would be added later?

A: No. We didn't want to inhibit him whatsoever. We wanted him just to be natural. If you look and study Michael Jordan's movement, he's like a gazelle. The pure nature of his body as animation itself is spectacular to watch because of his athleticism. So you don't want to inhibit that. Just do your thing, Michael.

Q: How was it done differently before?

A: With [optical] technology, you really couldn't shoot with a "wild" camera. You would do everything with a motion control camera. It would be on a track. You would program the [camera movement] and shoot that over and over again. Well, you can't really program Michael Jordan's moves because he's Michael Jordan. What he does with the basketball can't be repeated, and we can't repeat it photographically unless we have — as we've done in this case — built tools to allow us to then track his movement into any background or any environment that we want.

Q: It seems like a lot of studios are looking at technology like this now. Is this a trend?

A: Absolutely. What you're doing is creating images that tell better stories, so now anything is possible — no boundaries to what you create. Many more stories can be told because you can be that much more creative and experimental in how you tell them. It's hard for us illusionists to fool [audiences], because they are now educated. So they require much more sophistication visually as part of this moviegoing experience. This is the way movies will be made in the future.

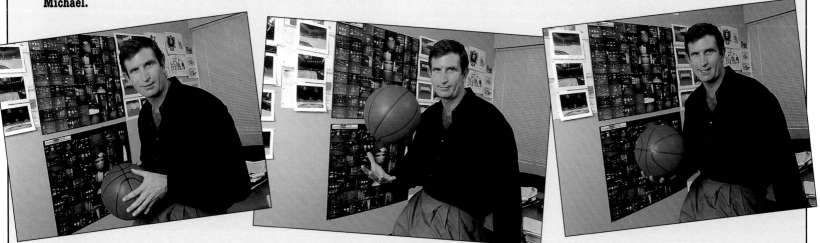

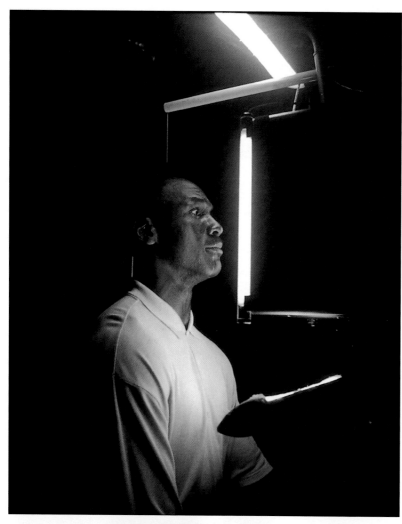

From real to reel

Cinesite's innovative technology allows it an edge in creating startling visual effects, and the studio has a hand in developing such technology. It's not so much what arrives on the screen that is drastically different from what has come before, but rather the ease of applying the technology. Speed, precision, and flexibility count as much as imagination in creating great visual effects. In a film like *Space Jam*, the goal is to use the technology in a subdued manner to tell a story. In doing so, the technological advances enhance rather than grandstand, giving the film a dimension that would have been impossible only a few years ago.

Michael Jordan is yanked into a hole on a golf course and pulled through a long tunnel into Looney Tune Land, stretching him to twice his normal height, the film's first big visual effect.

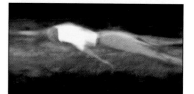

To achieve the squash and stretch cartoon effects with Jordan, the Cinesite team set up their equipment on the set and scanned him, giving every hill and valley of his face (and body) a numerical value. From this, a wireframe model of his head was created, and covered with computer "skin" in the same way the wireframe stadium was decorated with computer-generated surface materials. From this model, Jordan could be stretched like rubber and, in one scene, wadded up and bounced like a ball.

Play ball

The actual ball used in *Space Jam* was hand-delivered to Cinesite, where for three days it was scanned into a computer. Every smudge, mar, and scratch was accounted for digitally, and in nearly three dimensions, as it existed on the real ball. It could be programmed to move like a real ball, that is, spin in the air and roll on a bounce, so that visually there is no difference between it and its four-dimensional counterpart. Through clever editing, the animated players could freely pass to or steal from (less likely) Michael Jordan, who is always in possession of the real ball.

There are many images at work in this single frame of Marvin the Martian, one of tens of thousands of similar frames composited by Cinesite.

Some Cinesite test shots show possible ways to render the ball for the scene in which the NBA players get their skills back. Notice the changes in lighting on Michael Jordan's and Wayne Knight's faces. The effect above is closest to the one chosen for the film.

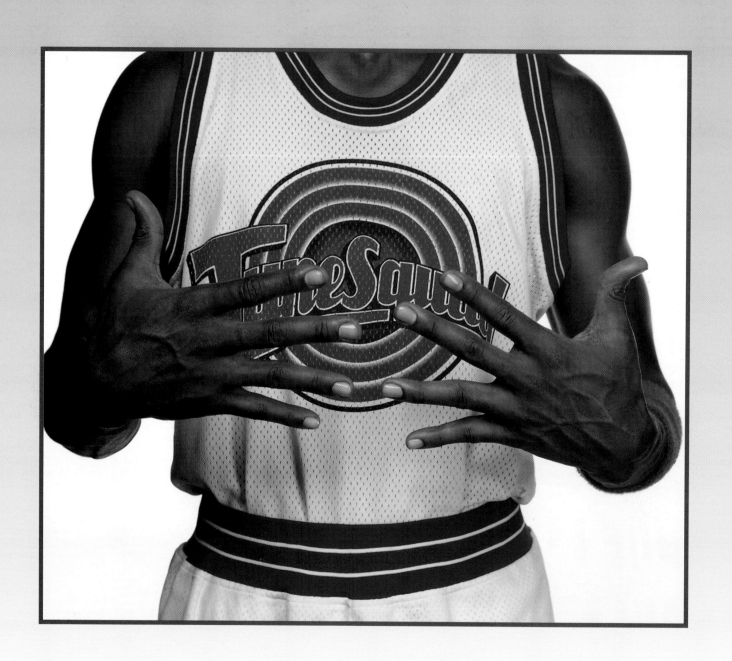

6

FINAL BUZZER

The animation is finished. The computer effects have blended the real with the unreal. The musical score is written, and a million last-minute details are being tended to. While the midnight oil burns and the release date becomes *real*, the producers realize, "Hey! We've got a movie!"

Final Frames

After months of hard work, the diverse elements of *Space Jam* begin to fold together into a single, unified work. At *Space Jam* Animation, with four months till the movie's opening, rough animation is finally complete, being cleaned up at a furious pace. One of animation producer Ron Tippe's main objectives is to match the energy levels between the late shift and the early one, and between studios in a spectrum of time zones. At the same time, the Cinesite crew works full-time on the scenes as they are handed off to them for compositing.

The studio's advertising and publicity machine, throttling up for its media bombardment in the fall, unveils its "teaser" campaign featuring striking silhouettes of Michael, Bugs, and the entire animated cast. "Get ready to jam" the posters declare, although the statement seems fairly absurd to anyone standing in the midst of the ambitious production, which has been "jamming" for a year to turn around a picture that would normally take twice that time. A pleased Ivan Reitman says wearily, "Bottom line: We're on track, and I'm surprised."

Last-minute edits, screen credit treatments, the theatrical trailer, advertising campaigns, and a myriad other dizzying issues demand split-second decisions of the production team. "This is the final rush. I wouldn't say it's tense, but it's a bit frenetic," Reitman admits. "There are a thousand little details that need taking care of at this stage, and if one of them is forgotten, you'll see it up on the screen." He swiftly corrects himself. "Maybe *you* won't, but *I* will."

"I want to stand up and cheer," he exclaims after watching the day's rough animation, as well as some "re-dos" or fixes of earlier shots. "This stuff looks amazing — the movie actually works!" he jokes. The months of hard work are starting to give hints of a payoff, although at the end of each of the dailies, Reitman applies more pressure to the production team. "I need more color shots. How come we don't have more finished sequences?" he pleads.

The pressure has had an indirectly invigorating effect on Ron Tippe and his animation

Working from his own scripted audio "blueprint," sound designer Mark Mangini creates the chuff-chuffing train sound of Swackhammer smoking a cigar.

staff. "[Ivan] has set the standard; he's pushed us to make a better movie," Tippe says. "Where another filmmaker is willing to say 'it's fine,' Ivan is not. He's pushing us to see the film not as a piece of animation but as a *whole* film." Tippe's crew is now in overdrive, with artists working in round-the-clock shifts to meet the movie's delivery deadline.

The deadline. From this point on, everything will be framed in its shuttering iris. Today, in separate studios just a few minutes from Warner Bros., the sound effects and musical scores are being created and recorded.

Even if you have never heard of a *zurrup*, a *trombone gobble*, or *comic boids*, chances are you have actually *heard* them. These are the stock-in-trade of an animation sound effects designer, a creator of noises that exist only in the fanciful world of cartoons. There are sounds of the real world, of course, which should sound real. Then there are sounds in the animated world, which should sound real and *then* some. Movie sound has gone from mere effects — recreations and caricatures of sounds — to full sound design, subtle and brash, evocative and manipulative. Today, a sound designer has nearly limitless options, mixing, warping, digitally sampling, and creating from scratch a broad auditory library. In today's movie business, sound is science; like a scent, it provokes an instant gut reaction.

"Sound can have a profound effect on how the audience perceives a film," explains Mark Mangini, founder of Weddington Studios in North Hollywood. "The sound designer's real challenge," he continues, "is to learn to read and feel the dramatic beats within a film and create sound to support them . . . to find connections or to break them, to create harmony or discord, to soothe or upset, to excite or reassure." Mangini should know of what he speaks: his sound creations for *The Lion King, Speed, Robocop,* and *Raiders of the Lost Ark* have won him Academy Awards. In fact, his Oscar-nominated fork-and-knife scene in *Aladdin* spawned the term "sound sculpting." At his mission control-style soundboards, Mangini will have put nearly eight months into *Space Jam*'s sounds by the time it is released.

"We wanted brand new, fresh basketball sounds, so we rented a local YMCA gym and [brought in] four or five guys — the sound artists. There were a bunch of players making slam dunks and we put microphones right into the baskets. We put mikes on the floor so we could get some really nifty sneaker squeaks. Put the mike at the chest, and you get some nice catching and passing sounds. We've got all sorts of new sounds," he enthuses.

Just as the Looney Tunes' sound effects are as identifiable with the spirit of the cartoons as the characters themselves, so too is the music. The bulk of it was composed

(top) Mangini peruses his computer listings for the right "trombone gobble." A quarter of the movie's sound effects are from the old Looney Tunes cartoons, another quarter created from scratch. The rest are available from existing sounds, catalogued and digitally stored in his studio computers. Using the script as a blueprint, Mangini breaks it down scene by scene, plugging in his needs for specific sounds.

and conducted by Carl Stalling, from the 1930s till his death in the 1950s. Stalling's music is used as a "scratch" (or temporary) track for portions of *Space Jam* to test its suitability and create a sense of tone in the early cuts of the film (this version of the film was screened for studio personnel; a "scratch track" never reaches the ears of a movie audience). Some of it seems curiously anachronistic in places. The producers, especially Reitman, are insistent that the movie has a contemporary tone, bringing the Looney Tunes into the 1990s, but Stalling's music is, in moments, simply too far out of its time. Fortunately, noted film score composer James Newton Howard, enlisted into the project a year earlier, had plenty of time to research the musical textures needed for the movie. The fact that Stalling's work, revered by most cartoon fans, lacked the energy to drive some portions of *Space Jam*'s animation is "interesting to see" for Howard, but not alarming. He remedies the problem by "trying to do some kind of hybrid with a Carl Stallingesque influence, but with a more contemporary kind of approach to it," he says.

(top) Artie Kane conducts the ninety-nine-piece orchestra assembled to record the *Space Jam* score. (above) In the engineer's booth, a pensive James Newton Howard, flanked by orchestrator Brad Dechter (left) and recording engineer Shawn Murphy, listens to his musicians before making suggestions for changes.

Howard's ninety-nine musicians gathered this morning in the cavernous Todd-AO Studios soundstage have never seen or heard the music before, relying instead on their masterful sight reading skills. Handed the score, they perform it cold, testing their chemistry, reaching for the music's style, its tempo, and its flavor. In contrast to the sophisticated technology used to create the film's visual effects, the scoring is perhaps the most organic element of *Space Jam*: no synthesizers, no computers, only pure music, drawn from acoustic instruments.

A deafening silence falls over the proceedings moments before the orchestra is to begin the first cue of the day, the scene of Michael Jordan being sucked into the golf hole. Each musician wears a headpiece that transmits a "click track" which keeps cadence with a rhythmic clicking, and counts out the seconds before they are to begin: click, click, click, and the music explodes in a clear and resonant and sweetly harmonious sound. Howard, in the control booth, watches the video monitor as much with his ear as his eye. The cue finished, the musicians await his comments. To the untrained listener, everything sounds perfect: melodious, unified. Howard, tall and as lean as his direction, has a more precise idea of what he wants.

"The snare drum is a little hot and I need to hear more from the xylophone," he says cordially. "I'd like to get a little more out of the tubas, and trombones three and four, and the bassoon." Howard directs his comments to conductor Artie Kane through a remote microphone. Kane, alone on an elevated stage, passes them along to the musicians.

Scoring a film is an exacting process. The notes and pauses between must precisely complement the visual pacing and rhythm of the film. Without music and sound, the film's emotional crescendos — missing a vital dimension — go flat.

There is an air of congeniality and crisp professionalism throughout the session. Difficult cues are handled first, while the musicians are still fresh. "This is my first animated feature, and I'm catching [punctuating] a lot more of the action than I would in a live-action film," Howard explains. "It's different in every way."

Simultaneously, in recording studios all over the country, demos for the movie's soundtrack (which will be released as an album in conjunction with the film) are being created like a great audio jigsaw puzzle. Ken Ross and Warner Bros. Music president Gary Le Mel have enlisted a twelfth-hour roster of writers, producers, and music superstars such as Brandy, R. Kelly, D'Angelo, and Monica to record original and cover songs, most with a broad and distinctive urban/pop flavor. Ross, Reitman, Le Mel, and Howard sift through the submissions and make their choices based on the "fit" for the film. In test edits, film editor Sheldon Kahn cuts the scenes to the songs to see how they play. Most of the songs are being written specially for *Space Jam*, some tailored to the tempo and theme of a specific spot in the film, while others are chosen because they seem to fit, as they are, in another spot. This song "spotting" process, part of the scoring of the film, is a huge endeavor, with decisions about the role a song should play being difficult and subjective. Ross solicits Michael Jordan's opinions informally after the initial choices are made. "Michael's got a keen sense for the music and wants to hear all the stuff," Ross says.

While the soundtrack is recorded over the next few days, there is a sense of relief at *Space Jam* Animation as the rough animation is completed. There is still much to do. All the elements, so nerve-wrackingly distrait only a few weeks ago, are now coming together quickly. Even so, no one is allowing for any surfeit of patience just yet. A short trailer, previewed at Warner Bros., draws big laughs at Bill Murray and the Looney Tunes, and an intense interest in Jordan's performance, as well as awe at the finished images — few as they are — which have a startling visual power and grace. Everyone involved with the film, from the decision makers in the conference rooms to the clerk in the consumer products department, is caught up in the excitement of a film that actually needs no promotional spin.

A freak thunderstorm visits Chicago the day the Bulls win their fourth NBA championship at United Center, soaking the city and cooling off the early summer heat. The Bulls are something of an extended identity for many of the city's residents, a throng of which gathers on the street outside Michael Jordan's restaurant. Cheers. Hoots. Car horns. Police press the crowd out of traffic, which circumnavigates the block like a parade stuck in a cul de sac. They've been ready for days. They are calm, restrained. They're fans, too. Inside the restaurant, one of Jordan's employees, her hand delicately calming a quivering lip, silently watches a monitor as an intrusive news camera stares at her boss. Caught in a struggle with the complex chemistry of joy and grief, Jordan isn't allowed a moment's privacy.

In Los Angeles, it's still daylight, and the night is young. Studio executives are elated. Celebrations are in order. It wasn't just a Bulls win. It was a *Space Jam* win, too. Jordan *had* returned to basketball, his status and form intact.

Meanwhile, Sheldon Kahn, Reitman's editor, continues to time the live-action footage, cutting and recutting (digitally, of course —

the days of the "cutting room floor" are a quaint movie footnote), fine tuning the movie's gags. For Cinesite's use, Kahn — using suggestions from the animation producer and co-directors — has cut the green screen material to no more than one extra frame at the beginning or end of a sequence (called a "hand-off"). This requires a keen eye and an extraordinary sense of timing on the part of the editor. Because compositing at Cinesite is an expensive, frame-by-frame process, no more material is used than is absolutely needed, down to the frame. On this day, the crucial material is footage to be used in the newest retake on the theatrical trailer, quick snips of film that convey the gist of the story at a brisk pace. It, too, will be tested for audience reactions, part of the arcane process of selling a movie.

"The thing that makes me most nervous at this point," Reitman says of the final weeks, "is that this is the very first comedy that I've ever worked on that we will not be able to prescreen for audiences. I've never released a comedy without previews, without some audience seeing it. I'm hoping we'll have enough by the end of September to be able to show it then."

The lights stay on late in the advertising and publicity offices. In the animation and Cinesite offices, too. Last-minute details are still being discovered and tended to. People aren't losing sleep so much as they are sacrificing it.

In the morning, there is talk in the halls of *Space Jam* Animation about *Space Jam II*, but it's water-cooler conversation so far. A sketch of Bugs, alarmed at the news from his wristwatch, reminds everyone that the release date is closing in. The halls are a muted bustle, quiet except for the sound of a copy machine. A fax is coming through. In the employees' pantry, someone is making popcorn.

As director Joe Pytka and Ivan Reitman begin to see final merged images of animation and visual effects, their excitement radiates through the whole production. Any concerns about whether the visual effects could be pulled off evaporate. Michael, Bugs, and cast are here, together on the big screen, with no seams showing.

The reel thing

When it was first announced that Michael Jordan was making a movie with the Looney Tunes, people said, "What a great idea," but there were concerns. Although he's known for being a naturally funny man, there was, nonetheless, endless speculation about his ability to translate his skills and instincts from the court to the screen. The difference with Jordan, according to his director, is his "internal discipline and incredible focus."

"Directing is easy compared to acting," insists Joe Pytka. "Acting is the most difficult thing there is. You're in front of the camera, exposed to the crew, exposed to the film, exposed to everything. Trying to perform, to be funny — whatever — is the hardest thing there is. My god, the pressure." At a screening of a rough cut of *Space Jam* for some Warner Bros. staff, ordinarily unimpressed audience members were overheard voicing their delight at Jordan's powerful screen presence. His unpretentious, understated self-portrayal, his charm and willingness to let himself be the butt of some very funny gags are enormously appealing. "For Michael to really come through [to audiences] well, plus do all the physical stuff, is truly remarkable," Pytka maintains. And how did he inspire Jordan to give such a performance? "I provoked him a lot," the director says, a hint of a smile bending the corners of his mouth.

Bugs Bunny goes Shakespearean on Michael Jordan as he tries to convince the star to get back into the game and help the Tune Squad defeat the Monstars. The teamwork Bugs needs to overcome enormous odds is reflected in the phenomenal *Space Jam* production team itself, as well as in Jordan's and the Chicago Bulls' astonishing 1995–96 season.

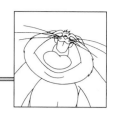

Interview

Q & A: Sheldon Kahn

March 3, 1996. Universal City, California. Sheldon Kahn has been Ivan Reitman's film editor for thirteen years, and was nominated for Academy Awards for his work on *One Flew Over the Cuckoo's Nest* and *Out of Africa.*

Q: Is this type of movie much more complicated for an editor than a strictly live-action film? There seem to be a lot more elements that can be manipulated.

A: It's unbelievably more complicated even though you can manipulate some of the things. On all the things shot against a green screen, we can change almost anything we want. We can make Michael Jordan smaller or larger, move him to the middle of the frame. Because Bugs Bunny was not shot on the set, I can do whatever I want with him. I can put him in a real tight close-up. I can make it a shot with four [live] people behind him, or Looney Tunes behind him.

Q: Instead of being stuck with the live-action footage that's already been shot ...

A: Right. [The] animation [team] is continually surprising me. They're just bringing this whole thing alive. Usually, when I work on a movie I know exactly what I've got: I've cut the scene, and I know exactly what it looks like. Then we go out and preview it. But by then, with the animation in, the picture is going to look absolutely brand new to me. I will certainly not have seen [the Looney Tunes] in color and finished off with the backgrounds and the polish. I'm going to go to the movie and go, "Wow! This is the first time I've seen it! It's wonderful!"

Q: It sounds like quite a different kind of film for you.

A: I'm going to be like a little kid, as opposed to knowing every frame of a picture like I normally do by the time it gets to preview. I can't wait for that, because there's a kind of magic about doing this kind of thing.

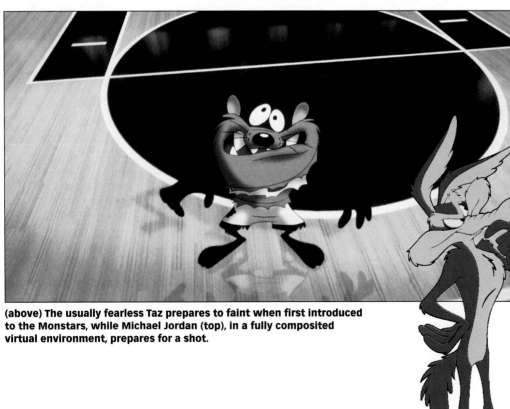

(above) The usually fearless Taz prepares to faint when first introduced to the Monstars, while Michael Jordan (top), in a fully composited virtual environment, prepares for a shot.

Interview

Q & A: Wile E. Coyote

March 23, 1996. Tyrone Guthrie Theater, Minneapolis, Minnesota. Wile E. is a coyote of few words, most of which he shared with us before a performance of his sell-out show, An Evening with Wile E.Coyote.

Q: What if your stage show had bombed?

A: How bad could it hurt? This is Wile E. Coyote you're talking to.

Q: Why did you do *Space Jam*?

A: Taxes. And I needed to stretch as an actor.

Q: This is a first for you — off the desert and not always chasing the Road Runner. What gives? Have you conquered your compulsions like so many other stars?

A: I'm in an anonymous program for predators.

Q: But now you're not anonymous.

A: I'm not serious, either. Next question.

Q: Do you have a favorite quote that sustains you during hard times?

A: "The greatest measure of genius is flexibility."

Q: Oscar Wilde?

A: Oscar Levant, I think. Or me. It all runs together, I'm afraid.

Q: While we're on the subject, what's your greatest fear?

A: Anything that requires assembly.

Sometimes, even a pep talk from Michael Jordan himself can't make Wile E. believe that what he's about to do is good for him. His instincts remind him that he's the exception to every rule, especially the ones relating to gravity and physics.

Michael Jordan, Wayne Knight, and their squash-and-stretch costars interact in a totally computer-generated environment, which at first looked *so* real the visual effects animators were ordered to make it look more cartoon-like.

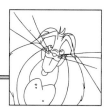

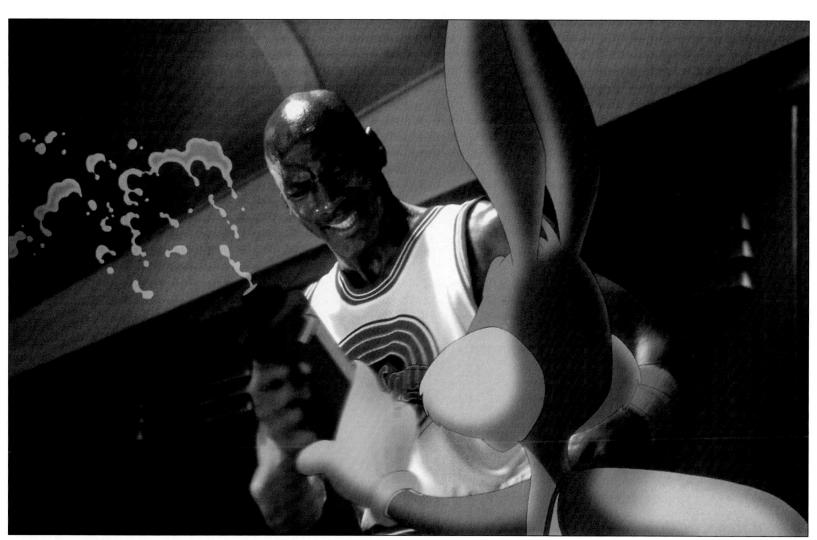

Bugs hands Michael his water bottle, which Bugs has cleverly altered to read "Michael's Secret Stuff." The benign elixir inspires the Tune Squad to face the Monstars in the game's tough second half.

Even the shadows on the wall of the Jordan children's bedroom are fully animated, then later composited by computer at Cinesite. (below) Bugs retrieves Michael's lucky North Carolina shorts from the superstar's home.

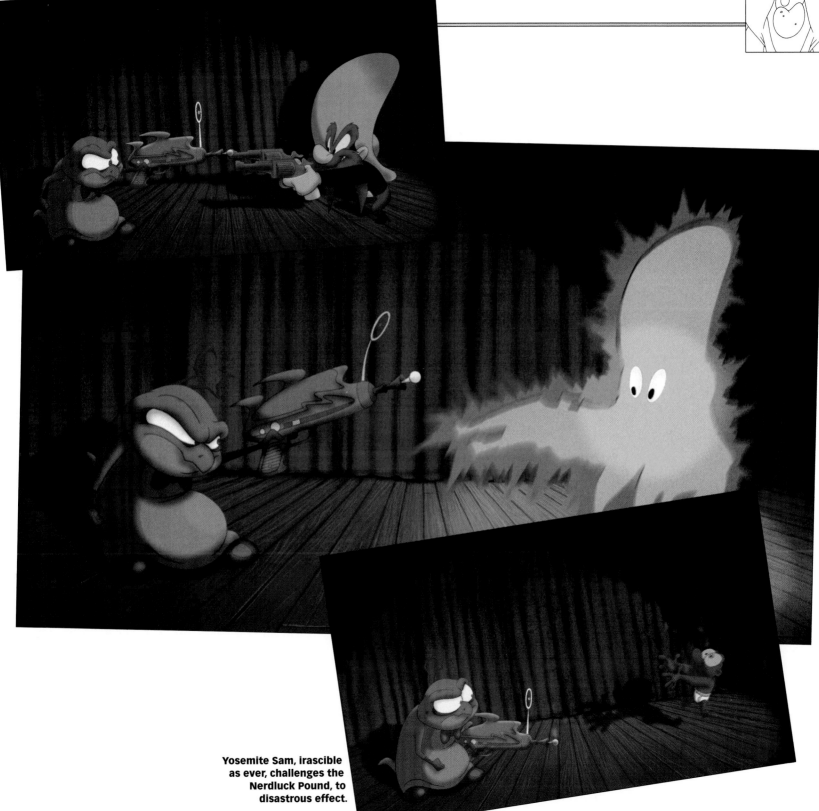

**Yosemite Sam, irascible
as ever, challenges the
Nerdluck Pound, to
disastrous effect.**

Porky Pig reacts to Michael Jordan's pep talk as Michael announces that they are going to keep playing, even though they are getting trounced.

Michael and the Tune Squad gather in a show of unity before the second half of the Ultimate Game. Each of these six characters was animated individually, and has up to seven layers of coloring, shading, and light sourcing, making a complicated shot for the compositer.

Lola shouts her encouragement to her teammates.

Within a virtual computer-generated stadium, Michael Jordan defends the Looney Tunes against the Monstars. The 25,000–member crowd is created with seven real people in costumes and masks, shot from different angles and computer multiplied and doctored to look animated, interspersed with animated foreground characters.

Art Credits

Title page Tweety by Tony Cervone and Allen Helbig

Page 11 Bugs Bunny by Allen Helbig

Page 13 Bugs Bunny (three poses) by Allen Helbig

Chapter One

Page 14 Bugs Bunny's eyes by
Allen Helbig

Page 15 Conceptual Bang Monstar by Bruce Smith and
Ashanti Miller

Page 19 Thumbnail sketches by Tony Cervone

Page 20 Conceptual Lola Bunny by Tony Cervone, Jeff Siergey,
and Ashanti Miller

Pages 22-23 The Looney Tunes by Tony Cervone and Allen Helbig

Page 24 Bugs Bunny by Tony Cervone, Doug Ninneman, and
Allen Helbig

Page 25 Daffy Duck by Tony Cervone, Jeff Siergey, Doug Ninneman,
and Allen Helbig

Page 26 Conceptual Swackhammer and Tweety by Uli Meyer
Conceptual Swackhammer with cane by Brian Smith
Conceptual Swackhammer with cigar by Vincent Woodcock
Conceptual Swackhammer with top hat by Dan Root
Conceptual Swackhammer in a tuxedo by Uli Meyer

Page 27 Conceptual Swackhammers by Vincent Woodcock
Conceptual Swackhammer with martini by Dan Root

Pages 28-29 Conceptual Swackhammer by Uli Meyer

Page 30 Bugs Bunny and conceptual Nerdlucks (top center) by
Tony Cervone

Bugs Bunny (hands spread) and conceptual Nerdlucks (top right)
by Harry Sabin

Conceptual Nerdlucks (center row) by Jeff Siergey
Conceptual Nerdluck (bottom left) by Vladimir Todorov
Conceptual Nerdlucks (bottom right) by Dan Root

Page 31 Conceptual Nerdlucks (top row) by Larry D. Whitaker, Jr.
Conceptual Nerdlucks (center row) by Paul Chung
Conceptual Nerdlucks (bottom left) by Uli Meyer
Conceptual Nerdlucks with guns (bottom right) by Paul Chung

Pages 32-33 Conceptual Nerdlucks by Paul Chung

Page 34 Conceptual Monstar in sneakers (top left) by Paul Fisher
Conceptual Bang Monstar head (top center) by Bruce Smith
Conceptual Bang Monstar head (top right) by Bruce Smith and
Tony Cervone
Storyboard sketch of Marvin the Martian, Elmer Fudd, and
conceptual Monstar (center left) by Martin Fuller
Conceptual Pound Monstar (center right) by Vladimir Todorov
Storyboard sketches of conceptual Monstars (bottom left and
center) by Uli Meyer

Conceptual Blanko Monstar head (bottom right) by Jeff Siergey and
Tony Cervone

Page 35 Conceptual Nawt Monstar (top left) by Jeff Siergey
Conceptual Monstars (right) by Bruce Smith
Conceptual Blanko Monstar head (bottom left) by Jeff Siergey and
Tony Cervone

Conceptual Blanko Monstar heads (bottom center and right) by
Tony Cervone

Page 36-37 Conceptual Pound Monstar by Bruce Smith

Pages 38-39 Final Nerdluck designs by Jerry Rees, Larry D. Whitaker,
Jr., Character Builders, Inc., and Uli Meyer Features Ltd.
Final Monstar designs by Tony Cervone, Jerry Rees, Jeff Siergey,
Bruce Smith, and Uli Meyer Features Ltd.

Page 40 Conceptual Lola Bunnies with basketballs (left and center)
by Gary Dunn
Conceptual Lola Bunny (right) by Rich Arons

Page 41 Lola Bunny models (all top left) by Tony Cervone,
Jeff Siergey, and Ashanti Miller (left) and Ashanti Miller (center
and right)
Conceptual Lola Bunny with hands under chin (bottom left) by
Tony Cervone
Lola Bunny thumbnail sketches (center) by Ashanti Miller
Conceptual Lola Bunny (top right) by Jerry Rees

Page 42 Michigan J. Frog by Allen Helbig

Page 44 Wile E. Coyote by Allen Helbig
Storyboard art by Kurt Anderson, Tony Cervone, and Jeff Siergey

Page 45 Road Runner by Allen Helbig
Storyboard art by Kurt Anderson, Tony Cervone, and Jeff Siergey

Page 46 Storyboard art by Kurt Anderson, Paul Hardman, Alex Mann,
and Joe Suggs

Page 47 Storyboard art (top row) by Harry Sabin and Bruce Smith
Storyboard art (center and bottom rows) by Harry Sabin,
Bruce Smith, and Kirk Tingblad

Page 48 Conceptual Moron Mountain planet (top left) by
Mark Whiting
Color script in photograph (bottom center) by Bill Perkins

Page 49 Conceptual Moron Mountain entrance (top center) by
Bill Wray
Color script panels (bottom center) by Bill Perkins

Page 50 Conceptual Moron Mountain Amusement Park (top right)
by Tass Darlington, Roy Naisbitt, and Tony Cervone
Conceptual Moron Mountain entrance (center left) by Dan McHugh

Pages 50-51 Conceptual Moron Mountain Amusement Park (bottom)
by Dan McHugh

Page 51 Conceptual Moron Mountain ride (top left) by Joe Suggs
Conceptual Moron Mountain ride (center left) by Harry Sabin